'Many churches across Europe ar[...] in decline or dying. We need t[...] the book of Acts that contribute[...] church. Matthew Porter reminds us that church is not an end in itself; the church points beyond itself to fulfil the mission of God by making disciples and planting churches. I highly recommend *Overflow* to everyone who wants to help the church thrive again by learning lessons from the church of Antioch for today.'

Dr Winfield Bevins, Director of Church Planting, Asbury Seminary and author

'That longing, that hunger, that thirst you and I have to see another move of God through the church – well, *Overflow* will quench some of it, because Matthew's words serve to excite and equip us as churches to live more like they did in Acts: in step with the Spirit.'

Anne Calver, Baptist minister, speaker and author

'It is always a joy to see churches structure ministry around the ministry of Christ described in Ephesians 4. In this book, Matthew Porter demonstrates visionary leadership that leads to a lived experience of the fullness of Christ, to what he calls "overflow". I heartily recommend this book to you.'

Alan Hirsch, founder of 100 Movements and 5Q Collective and author of numerous books on missional leadership, theology, and organisation

'This book is a great resource: great for reflecting on resource churches, but also a gift to those who want to reflect on church life in general. It is rooted in biblical reflection, draws on Matthew's extensive experience and wisdom, and offers concise insight that will encourage and stimulate in equal measure.'

Mark Tanner, Bishop of Berwick and author

'Matthew Porter embodies "overflow". As the leader of St Thomas' Newcastle, a Resource Church Plant sent by Matthew from The Belfrey, I know that Matthew lives out the foundations of overflow that he passionately lays out in this book. *Overflow* ends with a prophetic hope that church decline is not inevitable and that if we do the simple things of faith well, whole regions can be impacted by churches that overflow with the expectation that God is moving in our day. As you read this book, my prayer is that you, too, will develop a vision for overflow and that you will see how you and your local church can play your part in seeing our nation changed as we follow Jesus together.'

Ben Doolan, Leader of St Thomas', Newcastle, and Head of 18–30s Ministry for New Wine

'If you want to know more about the heart and vision of resource churches, this is the book for you. It's full of wisdom, inspiration and encouragement for all of us who long to see our region impacted for Christ.'

Lizzy Woolf, Team Rector, St George's Church, Leeds

'With the growing movement of church planting in England, *Overflow* makes an important contribution, focussing on lessons learnt from the church at Antioch. Biblically rooted and practically applied, this book will inspire leaders and teams of planting churches to prepare well and develop their effectiveness in planting churches strategically again and again.'

Ric Thorpe, Bishop of Islington and Lead Bishop for Church Planting in the Church of England

Matthew Porter is vicar/senior leader of The Belfrey in York, a vibrant Anglican church serving God's transformation of the north of England. He is pursuing doctoral studies in church planting at Asbury Theological Seminary. Matthew is author of *A–Z of Discipleship* and *A–Z of Prayer* and blogs in the fields of discipleship and leadership.

Matthew can be contacted by:
Email: matthew.porter@belfrey.org
Twitter: @matthewporteruk

OVERFLOW

Learning from the inspirational resource church of Antioch in the book of Acts

Matthew Porter

Authentic

First published 2020 by Authentic Media Limited,
PO Box 6326, Bletchley, Milton Keynes, MK1 9GG.
authenticmedia.co.uk

British Library Cataloguing in Publication Data
A catalogue record for this book is available from the British Library.
ISBN: 978-1-78893-125-0
978-1-78893-126-7 (e-book)

Cover design by Luke Porter
Printed and bound by CPI Group (UK) Ltd, Croydon, CR0 4YY

Contents

Foreword

Overflow is not another book of 'how to' methods of church leadership, although you will find much to equip you in Christian ministry within it. No, this is a book that catches what the Spirit is saying to the church at this time. It calls us to a renewed vision of the Christian life, and local church communities, overflowing with the life and grace of Jesus Christ. Understanding that this is the normal Christian life is a message that God has been bringing to his church through many voices. Now Matthew Porter calls us to take courage in the midst of the challenges of decline and lack of resources to look to the future with hope that God is pouring out a never-ending flow of his power and love and he is inviting us to step into this stream.

The first step into this overflowing life is to believe that it is possible and to begin to long for it. As Antoine de Saint-Exupery famously wrote, 'If you want to build a ship, don't summon people to buy wood, prepare tools, distribute jobs and organise the work, rather teach people the yearning for the wide, boundless ocean.'

In *Overflow* Matthew gives us a vision of a church and a life in God to long for that is characterised by boundless, overflowing love, joy, prayer, worship, and generosity. This vision comes from a rich engagement with the life of the church in Antioch from the book of Acts. Whenever God does a new thing, it is always a 'new-old' thing in which he reminds his people of who he is and what he has done before, and then says 'let's do it again'. The logic of Acts being included in the canon of Scripture must be that it is written to show us what the church in the power of the Spirit looks like. While we cannot be prescriptive in trying to copy what we read there, because of its unique time and context, I am convinced that it is more than simply a descriptive historical record. Instead it is instructive, giving us a vision to long for and principles to apply and learn from. Through it the Holy Spirit is saying to the church 'it can happen again'. And it is happening. I have the privilege of knowing something of Matthew's story and The Belfrey where he is vicar. I know that this is his lived experience and the stories he shares release faith that this is the life God has for us all and it is happening today.

Once we have begun to believe that this is possible, we then ask the question 'Yes but how?' This is a work of the Spirit and yet there are patterns and principles that we need to understand in order to partner with the Spirit's work. In John chapter 7 we read how Jesus described the overflowing life he was inviting his followers to live; 'Jesus stood and said in a loud voice, "Let anyone who is thirsty come to me and drink. Whoever believes in me, as Scripture has said, rivers of living water will flow from within them." By this he meant the Spirit, whom those who believed in him were later to receive' (John 7:37–39).

It all starts with the filling of the Holy Spirit and, as with everything that is filled, this starts to flow over the brim. This was the early church's experience from day one at Pentecost as the newly filled believers could not be contained within the upper room but spilled out into the streets. The gift of the Spirit was never given simply for the benefit of the individual believer. Too often the charismatic movement has reduced the Holy Spirit to personal experience. He was given to equip believers in seeing the kingdom of God come on earth. As the leaders in the New Wine family, who mentored me in the life of the Spirit, would often say 'The Holy Spirit is in you, and he wants out'.

It reminds me of a quote from Francis of Assisi: 'There are beautiful, wild forces within us. Let them turn the mills inside and fill sacks that feed even heaven'. The issue is not that the Holy Spirit lacks power or creativity or that he is absent – he is the wild force within us. The issue is whether we are filled and overflowing with his life and grace. As I prepared to write this foreword I met with K.P. Yohannan, the Metropolitan of the Eastern Believers Church in India. This church has seen more than 1.2 million people come to faith in Jesus Christ in the last few years and is currently planting an average of fifteen new churches every day. When I asked him about how this is happening, he said 'we don't tell people to plant churches it just comes from the overflow of God in our lives'. This is what *Overflow* is all about. But KP does train his leaders and members because, while this is a work of the Holy Spirit, it requires our participation. Matthew brings insight into how to take principles from the early church and apply them in our context. Understanding spiritual practices, what John Wesley called 'the means of grace', that sustain us in the fullness of the Holy Spirit and allow his grace to flow outwards is key. And fresh patterns of leadership are needed. Much has been written on the five-fold leadership gifts of Ephesians 4:11: apostles, prophets, evangelists, pastors and teachers. Too often what has been written has been technical and organisational. *Overflow* puts flesh on these dry bones and brings to life each gift and helps us to see their contribution to the life of the body of Christ.

My overwhelming emotion as I read *Overflow* was joy. I think that was partly the Holy Spirit rejoicing with my spirit in what I was reading because it is the life we are called to. And it was joy that this is possible, releasing fresh faith in me to believe and live for this again. The joy of the Lord strengthens us and we are going to need his strength if we are to see his church renewed and transformed into the overflowing life he is inviting us into. May this be your experience as you read this timely word to the church.

John McGinley
New Wine Head of Church Planting Development and author

Preface

This book is for anyone who wants to see their church have an overflowing impact on their surroundings. As well as church leaders, it's also for small-group leaders, leadership team members and church council members. In fact, it's for anyone with any influence in any local church. It's for those who want to play a part, however big or small, in seeing churches renewed and society transformed.

In these days when there is much talk of *resource churches* – that is, local churches which exist to influence their region by growing and planting on a regular basis – this book finds a clear biblical example of such a church in Antioch described in the book of Acts, and provides suggestions about things we can learn from that church today.

I don't think the ideas in this book are novel or unique. But they are timely. For there is surely a huge need for the contemporary church to rediscover its missional roots, to seek God for a refilling of his Holy Spirit and as a result overflow with love and kindness to others. One of the last times we saw such an overflow happening across the region where I live – the north of England – was in the 1860s, when a fresh awakening of the Holy Spirit was taking place in a number of parts of the world. At that time many men and women across Yorkshire and Lancashire surrendered their lives to Christ as a result of the faithful preaching of bold and brave evangelists and preachers. Not only were individuals and families affected but lots of new churches and chapels were planted, impacting many a village and town in the north. One man converted to Christ during that revival was my great-great-grandfather, Benjamin Porter. Benjamin married Anne, and their son, William, also followed Jesus. William married Arabella, and their son, Luther, also followed Jesus. Luther married Mary, and their son, Richard, also followed Jesus. Richard married Christine, and their son, Matthew (i.e. me!) also followed Jesus. So I am the fifth generation of Christ-follower flowing from that revival. All these years later, I am a living example of the ongoing influence of the church of that day. Such is the legacy of overflow! It impacts not just the church and society of the present, but also future generations too. For these reasons and more, we need, in our day, churches of overflow. Good churches. Strong churches. Missional churches. Spilling out with the good news of Christ.

I believe it's time. It's time again, for overflow.

My prayer is that this book will encourage, challenge and equip more churches in the twenty-first century to pray, work and learn to become churches of overflow.

Matthew Porter

Acknowledgements

A big thank you to:

The people of The Belfrey in York. You are graciously and often sacrificially putting into practice so many of the things written about in this book.

Sandy Millar, Nicky Gumbel and wider community of Holy Trinity Brompton (HTB), London. You've sought to create an overflowing church and I want to honour you for all you've been pioneering in London and in our nation.

My brothers Daniel, William and James. You're all men of overflow, having in your hearts a God-given desire to influence the world – Daniel through medicine and William and James through the local church. You are all such an inspiration to me!

Ric Thorpe. You live for overflow. Thank you.

My wife, Sam. You overflow with love and loveliness, patience and prayer.

To Jesus Christ. Spreading your fame and honouring your name are the reason for this book. May your overflowing kingdom come.

Introduction

overflow
verb

1. flow over the brim of a container
2. be excessively full or crowded
3. (overflow with) be very full of an emotion

I was surprised by what Luis Palau said. It was 2017 and I was at a church planting conference in the north-west of England, in Salford. Luis, now in his early eighties, was sharing some key insights he'd learned over the years which he was keen to pass on to the next generation. Having known that this great evangelist had been used by God to help hundreds of thousands of people put their faith in Jesus, I listened attentively. I expected him to tell us some exciting stories of people converting to Christ and that we'd then be urged to be courageous in telling people about Jesus. Instead, Luis gave a less passionate but more thoughtful presentation, painting a bigger picture of how communities are changed through a combination of evangelism and church planting. As people find faith in Christ, so churches grow, new churches are started and society is impacted. Luis told us that since he was a young man, he'd always believed that evangelism and church planting *go together* and that he saw his evangelistic ministry within the bigger work of church planting, influencing regions and nations. As he spoke, I was stirred. I sensed the

Spirit of God speaking to me about the Lord's desire to impact *my* region and nation! It was a holy moment as I felt again the prophetic call of God. From deep within I found myself praying the great prayer of Habakkuk: 'Lord, I have heard of your fame; I stand in awe of your deeds, Lord. Renew them in our day, in our time. Make them known.'[1]

Can this happen? Can local churches transform regions? I believe they can. Because I see examples of it in the Bible, signs of it across the world and glimpses of it here in the UK. It happens through churches of overflow.

> Can local churches transform regions?

Overflowing church

Many think of church as a building. Or an institution. Or an organisation. While church is sometimes those things, they're not at the heart of what it is to be church. Church, in essence, is people. Followers of Jesus in community. Disciples of Christ together. Church is followers of Jesus, full to overflow with his Spirit, spilling out in all sorts of ways so that others start following Christ and society is transformed.[2]

When followers of Jesus today are asked to consider an example in the Bible of this kind of transformative church, many think about the church in Jerusalem (in Acts 1,2) where it all started, or perhaps one of the churches to whom St Paul wrote – like the church in Rome, Ephesus or Colossae. But as I've read the New Testament again and again over recent years, there's a church that's stood out for me as an exciting example of a community that had an overflowing impact in its region.

It's the church of Antioch.[3] If I'd been alive 2,000 years ago, it's the Antioch church that I'd like to have been part of!

We're given wonderful glimpses into the Antioch Church in the Bible by Luke, the author of Acts of the Apostles. He shows us a community filled to overflowing with the Holy Spirit. Although we'd like to know more, there's still much to observe and from which to learn. This book shares some biblical insights into things we've been discovering about the Antioch church at St Michael le Belfrey Church in York (referred to mainly in this book by our short name, The Belfrey). I'm not writing as an expert or because we've achieved great success at The Belfrey. We've had some tough times and there's much we're still learning. We're not yet seeing the growth I believe the Lord intends, and we're only in the early days of church planting. But we are convinced of one thing – that the God and Father of our Lord Jesus Christ is a God of overflow, who invites us to give away what he gives. That's the way of impact. The way of growth. The way of blessing. The church in Antioch discovered this too, and provides a compelling example of a local church changing its region.[4] It's a church of overflow, impacting well beyond itself.

Prophetic and aspirational

So this book considers the Antioch church as an example of a church of overflow – as a model of a resource church. I will share some stories of what we've been learning and how this may help the church in the UK, Europe and beyond reach out in mission and see many come to Christ. As such, this is a prophetic book.

It's part of our offering to the wider church to consider, test and learn from. We are still discovering so much and our missional thinking is being stretched and changed as we learn from our successes and failures. Some parts of the book are aspirational, as we see areas into which the Spirit is calling us, but we recognise our fragility and lack of experience. Often it's when we work in our area of greatest weakness that God's strength is displayed and we see the greatest kingdom impact. There is much we don't know, but also there's much that the Holy Spirit is doing and revealing. What we do know is that we're called to overflow with the presence and power of God into our locality and region with all the resources God gives, as we learn from the Scriptures and from the example of churches like the church in Antioch.

> **We're called to overflow with the presence and power of God.**

Church in Antioch

So what do we know about the church in Antioch? This community of believers is mentioned in eight passages of the Bible:

Acts 6:5
mentions Nicholas 'of Antioch' – one of the seven specially chosen to serve at tables;

Acts 11:19–30
is the first reference to the Antioch church, where four phases of growth are identified;

Acts 12:25 – 13:3
describes a community of prophets and teachers in Antioch, and Barnabas and Saul[5] are sent out on a missionary journey

4

(Paul's so-called First Missionary Journey) from there, in the context of worship, prayer and fasting;

Acts 14:26 – 15:4
records the return of Barnabas and Paul and then their subsequent sending to Jerusalem for an important council of the church;

Acts 15:30–41
explains what happened when they returned from Jerusalem and how Paul and Barnabas had a disagreement and went on different mission trips (with Paul beginning his Second Missionary Journey);

Acts 18:18–23
describes Paul's return to Antioch (followed by Paul's Third Missionary Journey);

Galatians 2:11
describes Paul saying he opposed Peter when he came to Antioch;

2 Timothy 3:11
is where Paul, in passing, describes suffering and persecution while in Antioch.

These are the texts on which this book is based.[6] From them we're given significant insight into the life of a vibrant, Spirit-filled church which influenced not just its own community but its *region*. That's because the church in Antioch was a church of genuine overflow. It's why this book has the short and simple title: *Overflow.* It describes characteristics, structures and strategies that any community of Christ-followers desiring to reach out beyond themselves can adopt. If you want your church to become a church of overflow, do read on, and also consider the questions at the end of each chapter. Some of these questions are for individual readers while the five chapters relating to the five-fold ministry of apostles, prophets, evangelists, pastors and teachers also include questions to help start activating these gifts in others.

PART ONE

FOUNDATIONS FOR OVERFLOW

Small Beginnings

Things that grow start small. We often forget this, but it's true. Be it chives, children or churches, things that grow don't start life big. God has designed the world in such a way that living things normally begin with tiny seeds that don't look particularly promising. Yet in that seed is all the potential needed for something fine and strong to develop. This was true of the church in Antioch in the first century AD.

Antioch was a city on the eastern end of the Mediterranean, north of Israel in what was then called Syria. Founded near the end of the fourth century BC, sixteen miles inland and built next to the Orontes River, Antioch was the third largest city in the Roman Empire and a significant trading centre. Now a ruin, it lies near the modern-day city of Antakya in the south of Turkey. It was in this city that a new church community was planted. We read all about it in Acts 11:19–30 where we see four phases of initial growth.

Phase one: Early evangelistic work amongst the Jews (AD36–41)

> Now those who had been scattered by the persecution that broke
> out when Stephen was killed travelled as far as Phoenicia, Cyprus
> and Antioch, spreading the word only among Jews (v. 19).

God can use all sorts of things to start a church. The Antioch
church, probably begun around AD36, was formed because of
persecution. All followers of Jesus at that stage were Jews, based
almost entirely in Jerusalem.[1] The Jerusalem church, formed
six years previously, had been growing nicely until 'a great persecution broke out amongst the church in Jerusalem, and all
except the apostles were scattered throughout Judea and Samaria' (Acts 8:1). Some of these Jewish believers went to Antioch
and began telling other Jews about Jesus and as a result a small,
fledgling church of Messianic Jews was born.

This is all we know of this first phase of church life in Antioch. We're told nothing else. We don't know who the first
converts were, who its leaders were or what its characteristics
were – although it may well have been a mini-version of the
church in Jerusalem that we read about in Acts 2:42–47 and
Acts 4:32–35.

It's likely this church didn't look at first like it had great potential. Most churches are like this when they start. Few would
have guessed what the Antioch church would become and the
influence it would have.[2] But the Holy Spirit knew and sparked
into life this small new community of believers.

Today all sorts of new churches are being formed across the
world. I visited one in 2013 in Burundi, in East Africa. Ferdi-
nand, one of the pastors, introduced me to some of the new

believers and showed me the small church building they'd constructed on the hillside. He smiled as he told me that from this church they would soon plant a new community in the next village, and then the next and so on. 'I'm praying that in twenty years this church where we stand will be the cathedral – the mother church – of this area.' God had given him a vision of planting churches in his region and he was excited! He felt it was his destiny. I expect it is, as some six years on, many people have started to follow Jesus and a handful of new churches have already been planted. But let's not forget – it all starts small!

Jesus said just this in Mark 4:

> Again he said, 'What shall we say the kingdom of God is like, or what parable shall we use to describe it? It is like a mustard seed, which is the smallest of all seeds on earth. Yet when planted, it grows and becomes the largest of all garden plants, with such big branches that the birds can perch in its shade' (vv. 30–32).

Jesus wanted his followers to see the potential in the seed of his good news. Inside is everything needed for vast growth. It's so easy to miss this and see such seeds as insignificant. Seeds also take some time to germinate and grow. New seedlings are vulnerable and not all survive. But those that do can grow surprisingly large. But it all starts small. The Antioch church when it was first planted was not yet the overflowing church it would become, but it had all the potential to be, despite its small and humble beginnings. The Bible says, 'Do not despise these small beginnings' (Zech. 4:10, NLT). From 'these small beginnings' began one of the most significant churches of overflow ever to have existed. It's been left to us in the New Testament as a model and a guide of what a church of overflow might look like.

This was phase one of four phases of growth in the church in Antioch.

Phase two: New evangelistic work amongst the Greeks (AD42)

> Some of them, however, men from Cyprus and Cyrene, went to Antioch and began to speak to Greeks also, telling them the good news about the Lord Jesus. The Lord's hand was with them, and a great number of people believed and turned to the Lord (Acts 11:20,21).

We now jump ahead about six years. In the intervening period, the Holy Spirit had made clear to the church beyond Antioch that they were not just to reach Jews, but that non-Jews could and should also hear the good news (see the exciting story in Acts 10 of the conversion of Cornelius and his household in Caesarea). In Acts 11 we're told that this news reached Jewish believers in Jerusalem and no doubt beyond, too, with the result that Greeks began to follow Jesus as well. This affected the small church in Antioch, because believers from nearby Cyprus and Cyrene came and began to tell Greeks in the city how amazing Jesus was.

The Bible says that 'the Lord's hand was with them' in this missionary work – referring to God's hand of blessing.[3] The Lord honoured and prospered their evangelism as they shared the good news of Jesus to all in the city, not just to one people-group. While all disciples are obediently and continually to share the good news of Christ whether we see much fruit or not,[4] there are times when it feels like God is particularly helping the work and there is obvious and growing fruit. That's what was happening here, with the result that 'a great number of people believed'.

So, the Antioch church began to see significant growth when they began new evangelistic work with other ethnic groups. My friend Mark Miller, who leads Stockton Parish Church, noticed something very similar when a few years ago they opened their doors to Iranian asylum seekers in Stockton-on-Tees. From just one family and a single man eight years ago, many Iranians are now part of the church, most of whom have had life-changing encounters with Christ. Indigenous leadership has emerged with one already ordained and others in the pipeline. Through a warm welcome, faithful preaching and lots of love and care, a wonderful work of God is taking place![5]

It's interesting that in Antioch it took people from outside the city to start this new phase of growth. That's often the case. It sometimes takes new people, even new leaders with new vision, to enable a church to move from one phase of life to another.

> It sometimes takes new people, even new leaders with new vision, to enable a church to move.

When in 2000 I was invited to become vicar of St Chad's Church in Woodseats, Sheffield, the bishop and church council had recognised that it was time for a new phase of church life and they asked the new leader to help lead them into that. I was a young, rather naïve but nevertheless enthusiastic leader who helped take the church into a new season. Over nearly nine years we saw growth in numbers, in maturity, in finances and in community impact. It was not all straightforward or plain-sailing as the church changed significantly (and change is never easy!) but it was a good time, and it felt like 'the Lord's hand was with' us. This was particularly the case in Antioch in AD42. As we read of 'the Lord's hand' at work in this growing community we're not told of the growing pains, but there must have been many, especially as the church began to fill up with non-Jews – people who were culturally very different from the original church. While they were probably pleased to see the growth, we can imagine that this must have been tough for the original congregation of Messianic Jews who no doubt had lots of questions and at times would have found the changes difficult.

In this second phase of initial growth of the Antioch church, the result was not just good growth, but *large* growth! We're not told any figures, except 'a great number of people believed'.[6] This must have been exciting! Momentum picked up, as individual after individual and household after household encountered the risen Christ and became his followers. This was the start of what is sometimes today called *revival*.[7]

Revival is a sovereign outpouring of the Spirit of God, resulting in new followers of Jesus being made and the church growing. This normally results in social transformation as Christ-followers then bring positive change to their families, streets and communities. Throughout history, many great social advances have come as a result of revival.[8] Revivals have happened in many places over the last 2,000 years.[9] They are normally precipitated by a number of faithful disciples praying for God to pour out his Spirit. Indeed, this was what Jesus asked the disciples to do after his resurrection (see Acts 1) before the Spirit came in power in Acts 2. It's likely therefore that during the initial six years of phase one of the Antioch church, the small but faithful Jewish disciples cried out to God in prayer for his Spirit to fall in their city. If this was the case, God was now answering their prayers. The nineteenth-century evangelist D.L. Moody knew of this, which is why he said that 'every move of God can be traced to a kneeling figure'.[10] God loves to answer such faithful and persistent prayers.

This 'great number of people' who believed, which Luke refers to in Acts 11:21, are also described as having 'turned to the Lord'. That's a good and helpful phrase describing what elsewhere in the Bible is called *repentance*. Repentance is all about change. It means changing your mind with a resulting change of direction. Someone who's repented was once heading in one direction but now is going the opposite way. It's a simple but profound picture of coming to Christ and following him. It describes the decision to start a new life, receiving the new identity that Jesus offers, which is sealed in baptism. Repentance and faith go together.[11] People believe in Jesus and now follow him and his priorities, rather than any other agenda.[12] In this simple phrase, saying that 'people believed and turned to the Lord', Luke is concisely and helpfully describing the heart of conversion. The fact that it was happening to 'a great number of people' is a description of revival.

As we seek for a similar work of revival in our day and in our land, so we need to be praying and working to see many believing and turning to the Lord. In York, the city where I live, I'm praying that we would see people every day beginning to follow Jesus.[13] To be honest, I don't think we're seeing that yet, but I'm longing that we will. In the same way that the Lord did such things in places like Jerusalem and Antioch 2,000 years ago, and has done it in many other places since, so it is time for him to visit my city and my region in our day. 'Come, Holy Spirit' is my constant prayer.

So, from 'small beginnings' in phase one we find a good-sized and growing church by the end of phase two. But for the church to mature and begin to become a church of genuine overflow, a new phase of growth was needed, guided by new leadership.

Phase three: New leadership under Barnabas (AD43–45)

> News of this reached the church in Jerusalem, and they sent Barnabas to Antioch. When he arrived and saw what the grace of God had done, he was glad and encouraged them to remain true to the Lord with all their hearts. He was a good man, full of the Holy Spirit and faith, and a great number of people were brought to the Lord (vv. 22–24).

When the church in Jerusalem heard about the revival in Antioch, they would have been excited! They also would have wanted to make sure that all was going well. They knew from experience that such an outpouring of the Spirit needs good leadership[14] not to control, but to guide and lead. So they sent Barnabas.

Barnabas was the nickname of a man named Joseph.[15] He was probably called Barnabas – which means 'son of encouragement' – because he was a natural encourager. Some people are like that. While all Christ-followers are called to encourage, some just can't help bringing encouragement all the time. They exude encouragement! Barnabas had proved his leadership credentials in Jerusalem already. He had generously given the full proceeds of a field to the church and trusted the leadership with the money.[16] He had also been identified as being 'full of the

Spirit and wisdom' and so was chosen as one of seven to serve in the daily distribution of food to widows.[17] He was a Jewish man and, being a Levite – a priestly tribe – by birth, was already trained for leadership, and yet he'd been brought up outside Jerusalem, in Cyprus, where some of those who'd started the revival in Antioch had come from.[18] So it's possible he already knew some of those leading the Antioch church. As such he would have fitted in nicely in Antioch and was ready to lead.

It's noteworthy that there's no record that the leaders already present in Antioch became threatened by Barnabas's arrival. Maybe this was because his gift of encouragement smoothed the way with them and, as noted, his multiethnic background could have helped too. It's also probable that the leaders in Antioch needed genuine help and were straining under the pressures of growth, and so were pleased when Barnabas arrived. I'd like to think that he was welcomed and well-received.

As we've seen, a new phase of growth often requires new leadership from outside. That was the case now as the church entered phase three of its life. Church authorities today would be wise to learn from this – that although indigenous leadership is the norm and desire, it's not always what's needed in pioneering situations. Sometimes fresh leadership from outside is helpful. This new leadership should, however, tread wisely and carefully. This is what Barnabas does. He arrives, surveys what he sees and takes stock. As he does this, we're told that 'he saw what the grace of God had done' and 'he was glad'. He saw evidence of God's grace and he was pleased with what he saw.

> Grace is . . . a love that is undeserved, unconditonal and unending.

'Grace' is the biblical word for God's love. It's no ordinary love; rather, it's a love that is undeserved, unconditional and unending. It's seen supremely in Jesus Christ.[19] Barnabas knew that God loves pouring out this grace on people and that there is always more grace available. As he heard the testimony-stories of changed lives, he knew these were signs of grace. And the result was that 'he was glad'. His heart was stirred and moved and warmed. He became happy and (as we'll see more fully in Chapter 4) through his character and gifts, helped create a joyful church in Antioch that resulted in overflow.

As Barnabas took up leadership of the church in Antioch, what happened? We're told that 'a great number of people were brought to the Lord'. In essence, the church entered another period of significant growth and, as in phase two, this wasn't just a good number but 'a *great* number of people' (my emphasis). This really was starting to become a significant revival! The Spirit of Jesus was doing a work of real depth and establishing Antioch as an influential church. Barnabas would have known this work of God was for a purpose and that the Lord had greater plans for the city and region.

Growth and influence is God's desire for every church, but many churches fail to achieve their growth potential. There may be all sorts of reasons for this. One of the main jobs of leaders is to lead their church into growth. It was my privilege to play a part in this when I did my curacy training at Christ Church Dore in Sheffield in the late 1990s, and then as leader of St Chad's Church up to the end of 2008. I know from experience that this can at times be very difficult, especially if there are significant voices trying to lead the church in a different direction. Leaders need much prayer, help, strength, support and wisdom.

> Growth and influence is God's desire for every church.

Although the Antioch church needed Barnabas's wise leadership, there's no sense that he was the one who made it grow. Rather, he was more steering and nurturing the growth the Lord was bringing.[20] Good leaders know this. They know that they can try too hard. As well as under-leading they can over-lead and get in the way of the work the Lord is doing. Learning from his experience in the Jerusalem church, it's likely Barnabas would have sought to do the basics well and to encourage the people. He was a great choice for this, being such an encourager!

Phase four: Growth in discipleship under Barnabas and Saul (AD46–47)

> Then Barnabas went to Tarsus to look for Saul, and when he found him, he brought him to Antioch. So for a whole year Barnabas and Saul met with the church and taught great numbers of people. The disciples were called Christians first at Antioch.
>
> During this time some prophets came down from Jerusalem to Antioch. One of them, named Agabus, stood up and through the Spirit predicted that a severe famine would spread over the entire Roman world. (This happened during the reign of Claudius.) The disciples, as each one was able, decided to provide help for the brothers and sisters living in Judea. This they did, sending their gift to the elders by Barnabas and Saul (vv. 25–30).

As the church grew, Barnabas soon realised he needed particular help. He needed not just the aid of those already in the church, important though that was. He needed help from outside. The help of a specialist. And he knew exactly who he wanted.

Tim Keller, in his masterly paper *Leadership and Church Size Dynamics*[21] has helpfully shown that as a church grows it becomes increasingly important to bring in specialists with particular gifts. Keller also recognises that there's benefit in headhunting the person you want – someone not just with the gifts needed, but most importantly, the right character. Barnabas instinctively knew this. He wanted an excellent evangelist and teacher whom he could trust, and he could think of no one better than a man from Tarsus called Saul.

This is the same Saul whom the readers of Acts have been introduced to at the end of Acts 7 – who was present at and approved the stoning of Stephen and looked after the coats of those who murdered him.[22] It's the same Saul who in chapter 9 has a dramatic encounter with the risen Christ on the road to Damascus and receives an apostolic calling.[23] It's this Saul whom, by AD46, Barnabas thinks is the person needed in Antioch to help nurture the revival that's taking place.

There's a good lesson for leaders here, reminding us that we're not called to be 'Lone Rangers' and lead on our own. It's always about team. We need team. The right team. A complementary team. A unified team.

As we've sought to build team at The Belfrey, we recognised that it's best, if possible, to include a variety of gender, personality, experience and gifts in the mix. Our team balance may not always look precisely as we wish, but it's good to pray and ask the Lord for exactly the people on team that he desires, who will advance the apostolic mission of the church. This is what Barnabas was seeking when he went to find Saul.

Why Saul? It's probable that Barnabas was good at encouraging, nurturing and pastoring those who were already believers (see Chapter 4). He was also good at teaching (see Chapter 6).

What he required was another teacher to work with him, but also someone with other gifts too, particularly gifts of *evangelism*. He needed an evangelist (see Chapter 7) who could continue the work already taking place and train, strengthen and equip the church for further ministry and mission. Saul was the man he wanted. So, he went to Tarsus and found him[24] and brought him back to Antioch so that 'for a whole year' they together 'taught great numbers of people'. They poured out their gifts, time, energy and love into the Christ-followers in Antioch. It's probable (although not stated) that the church continued to grow in numbers and strength. What we certainly know is they 'taught great numbers of people'. We don't know exactly how they did this, but certainly God was establishing a strong and strategic work in Antioch, preparing it for the mission base it was to become. The Holy Spirit was pouring himself into this church, through Barnabas and Saul, so the church could then pour out into others. They were being prepared for overflow.

I wonder if Saul needed much persuading to go to Antioch. It's hard to know. He certainly was not frightened of travelling, hard work or opposition. During his significant God-encounter during his conversion, the Lord had called him to a work which he knew would be rewarding but difficult. He discovered this to be true straight away as he preached in Damascus but then had to escape for fear of his life. He then went to Jerusalem only to find that his preaching resulted in some wanting to kill him,[25] before he moved to Arabia.[26] It seems Saul then spent further time in Damascus and Jerusalem again before ending up back in his home town of Tarsus, where he stayed probably for around ten years, learning to preach the gospel, probably seeing some conversions and maybe even starting some churches.[27] It's in Tarsus where Barnabas found him in AD46. Maybe Saul had heard about the revival in Antioch and was pleased to be invited to join in. Certainly Saul and Barnabas already knew each other, and were probably friends, as it was Barnabas who bravely vouched for him soon after his dramatic conversion – when others were unsure of his authenticity – taking Saul to the apostles in Jerusalem.[28] So maybe Saul was pleased now to be invited to work in partnership with his old friend, now in Antioch. In any event, the work was so exciting and significant it must have been a wonderful and formative experience for both of them, as the Lord used them and developed them as disciples and leaders.

It was during this fourth phase of growth that the Antioch church had its first recorded experience of prophets and prophecy (see Chapter 5). Prophecy is saying what God says. It's sharing a particular word in season from God. Kris Vallotton, who has a significant prophetic ministry today, describes prophecy like this: 'God's voice is always around you; you just need to learn to "tune in" to His wavelength. To do that, you need the gift of prophecy, which will equip you to tap into the spirit realm that surrounds you even though you can't hear it with your naked ear. The gift of prophecy is like a radio received from Heaven.'[29] The Archbishop of York, John Sentamu says that 'God loves to speak to us. We need to be still and, like a radio, learn to tune in'.[30]

During this time when Barnabas and Saul were teaching great numbers of people, some prophets came from Jerusalem, sharing messages from God. One of them, a man called Agabus, accurately predicted that a famine was coming – which indeed came 'during the reign of Claudius'. As a result of this prophetic word, the Antioch church decided to collect a generous gift to help the church struggling in Judea, which Barnabas and Saul then took to the elders in Jerusalem.[31] So it's likely that, amongst other things, Barnabas and Saul had taught the disciples in Antioch to be generous. To give. When we give as a response to God's overflowing grace, the Lord gives more than enough, so we can give again (see Chapter 3). This is what Barnabas had seen in Jerusalem. It's what he'd been part of as he gave away his field. And it's what the Antioch church now did in response to the famine. They gave. The church in Antioch was now beginning to understand what it was to be an overflowing church.

The Antioch church didn't start off as a church of overflow. It took time as it grew, moved through various phases of church life and took on particular characteristics of overflow. In the coming chapters we'll look at some of these characteristics in more detail, beginning with one of its most basic but important features – being a people who prioritise worship, prayer and fasting.

Application: Growing a church of overflow

Questions for disciples and church leaders to consider from this chapter:

1. Which of these four phases of church life best represents where your church finds itself at present?

2. 'Do not despise these small beginnings' (see Zech. 4:10, NLT). Are there signs of 'small beginnings' in your church, or an area of work in which you're involved? How can you encourage growth?

3. Are you being called to a new church to lead (or help lead) them into a new phase of church life? What have you learned from the example of Barnabas, as he took the Antioch church into phase three?

4. Do you need to headhunt a specialist (like Barnabas found Paul) in order to help your church grow in discipleship and numbers?

5. What do you learn from the Antioch church, that will help you become more of a church of overflow?

Worship, Prayer and Fasting

In 2013, The Belfrey established a House of Prayer (HOP) in St Cuthbert's Church in York. The impetus for this HOP had come to me round our dining table in 2011, as my brother William shared with us one day over lunch what was happening at the Beacon House of Prayer in Stoke-on-Trent, which he and his wife, Karen, were leading. As William spoke, the Holy Spirit came on me and I sensed the Lord calling me, and The Belfrey – the church I lead – to establish a similar prayer centre in our city. Some eighteen months later, St Cuthbert's HOP was established, with a vision closely linked to that of The Belfrey, aiming to be *seeking God and his transformation of the north*. It's not insignificant that St Cuthbert's Church is named after the evangelist and church planter Cuthbert (c.634–687), a significant pioneering leader who brought the good news of Christ to the people of the north of England. Indeed, Cuthbert is sometimes described as 'the apostle to the north'. There's probably been a building for worship on the site of St Cuthbert's Church in York since the seventh century, so it may be that the first church was named after Cuthbert soon after his death. The site therefore has a rich heritage and is a great place in which to pray. Prayer seems easy there. Over the last few years, the HOP community has been crying out from that place for God's Spirit to be poured out in York and the north in our day. They've done this through worship, prayer and fasting.

Worship, prayer and fasting were also important 2,000 years ago in Antioch. We see this particularly in Acts 13:1–3, where we read:

> While they were worshipping the Lord and fasting, the Holy Spirit said, 'Set apart for me Barnabas and Saul for the work to which I have called them.' So after they had fasted and prayed, they placed their hands on them and sent them off (vv. 2,3).

So, we see in Antioch that these three disciplines of worship, prayer and fasting were part and parcel of their life as a church. It's what they did. It showed their love for Christ and their devotion to him.

The priority of worship

The overflowing church in Antioch loved to worship.

Worship, according the Bible, is expressed through our lips[1] and our lives.[2] Augustine of Hippo expressed it like this: 'Sing with your voices . . . Sing also with your conduct.'[3] Both are important. God loves to receive heartfelt worship, and we're called to spend time daily giving our adoration to him in this way. The Psalms are full of examples of this. But disciples are also called to a lifestyle of worship, which is about living in such a way that we are fully devoted to Christ. Paul in Romans 12:1,2 calls this being 'a living sacrifice, holy and pleasing to

God – this is your true . . . worship'. The overflowing church in Antioch expressed worship in both these ways. Here we focus especially on the first – on spending time in giving God our worship.

What we see in Acts 13 is the Antioch church giving time to 'worshipping the Lord' (v. 2). The Greek word used for *worship* here is the word '*leitourgeo*' which means to serve publicly in worship. We get the present-day word 'liturgy' from it. It's also the word used to translate the work of the Levitical priests in the Old Testament. Given this is what the *whole* church was doing, it reminds us that as New Testament believers we're *all* called to serve before the Lord in this way, not just a chosen few, as was the case for the priests in the Old Testament,[4] and that our offerings of worship are sweet and pleasant to the Lord.

When we worship we're showing our appreciation of God. We tell him how much we value him for who he is, and we give our thanks for all he's done and is continuing to do. We acknowledge that he is God, not us. We recognise that we belong to him, having been purchased by the death of Jesus and filled with his life-giving Spirit. We humble ourselves before him, lifting him high. We recognise that he is loving, forgiving, kind and generous. He is the God of overflow, the God described in Psalm 23 as 'The Lord is . . . my shepherd. I always have more than enough.'[5] He is worthy. No one deserves worship more than him. For there is no one like him. When we truly worship we become truly human, because we were made to worship. As such, worship is not about servile duty but heartfelt devotion. It's an expression not of obligation but of adoration. Not of law but of love.

> When we truly worship we become truly human, because we were made to worship.

27

At The Belfrey we love to worship. As we're a city-centre church and our doors are normally open during our services, we get all sorts of people wandering in. Often, they ask what's going on. Sometimes they ask if there's some special event happening, to which we normally reply that we're doing what we do whenever we gather, which is to give Christ our love and devotion. He deserves all our praise and worship!

God loves to receive our worship. It honours him and pleases him. He loves to respond to our worship and draw close to us, as we draw near to him.[6] That's why we often feel his presence as we worship. As the Holy Spirit is welcomed, he moves as we worship – touching lives, filling hearts, distributing gifts, bringing joy – as we fix our eyes on Jesus and boldly approach our good Father's throne. As we do that we're not rejected by God, but accepted. We're forgiven and welcomed. Affirmed and embraced.

These things are often experienced as we worship. That's why some people come to faith in Christ during worship. Or they get healed. Or encouraged. Or comforted. In the 1970s there was a woman in our church who would often have oil appear on her hands as she worshipped. Oil is a sign in the Bible of the presence of the Holy Spirit. Her hands would be visibly wet by the end of the worship-time. When she laid her hands on people who were sick, they were often healed.

All this and more can happen in the context of worship. It takes place in the simple and sincere act of giving God our thanks, praise and love. This is what they did in Antioch when they gathered: they worshipped. It's likely that this worship happened in different sizes of gathering – from the large to the small, as was the case in the Jerusalem and Ephesian churches.[7] They may have worshipped and taught outside, as well as in public buildings and in smaller settings, like homes. We're not told what they did when they worshipped, but if it was like what we see elsewhere in the Bible, it's probable that they sang songs (as Paul and Silas later did in the Philippi prison in Acts 16:25); that Scripture was read (as Timothy is told to do in 1 Timothy 4:13); that they listened to teaching (as we see in Acts 20:7); that the Lord's Supper was shared (as we read in Acts 2:42[8]) and that prayers were offered (as we see when the Jerusalem church gathered in Acts 4:23–31).

Worship should be the priority of every church. It's basic to what followers of Jesus do. It's a discipline that is an honour to practise. We tell the Lord how much we appreciate him. This means that our worship is God-directed and that he is addressed in our worship. I recently visited a church where God's name was not ever invoked during the service. The church was vibrant and contemporary, using the best of modern technology, but not once was God personally addressed or sung to. Something felt wrong. The focus was not upward towards God. Afterwards I realised that we'd gathered, but we'd not worshipped.

The significance of prayer

As the church in Antioch gathered, not only did they worship, but they also prayed. Prayer is communication with God.[9] As such, there is a great overlap between prayer and worship. It's not always easy to see where worship stops and prayer begins, or vice versa. That doesn't really matter. What's important is that we do both.

Some people find prayer hard. Talking with someone who can't be seen can be difficult. That's why we need to practise, day after day. It's often helpful to pray out loud, or with others. In fact, there are all sorts of ways you can pray. Whilst standing. Whilst kneeling. Whilst lying in bed. Whilst in the shower, or sitting on the toilet, or driving in the car, or walking down the street. We can pray any time, any place, anywhere. What's important is that we pray. Because prayer changes things.

> Prayer changes things.

Sometimes we see the results to our prayers; sometimes we don't. But if we keep praying and trusting, we will see more than enough answers to our prayers to encourage us to keep going, knowing that they really do make a difference. Over the years I've seen hundreds of examples of this. They include prayers for provision, protection and guidance, and much more. Some of these prayers have been answered with remarkable timing, and sometimes with an instant response.

In the summer of 2011, I misplaced my footing on a step whilst working in our back garden, turning my ankle. I heard a snapping sound inside the ankle-area followed by a shooting pain surging through from the back of my foot and up my leg. I collapsed to the floor in agony. I knew the damage was significant. Sam, my wife, was nearby and saw me fall and heard my cry of pain. I instinctively said to her, 'Sam, pray now! Speak healing over my ankle, in the name of Jesus!' – and she did. As soon as she prayed, the pain began to recede back down by leg and into my foot until within a few seconds it had totally gone. Sam helped me stand up, very cautiously. I was worried my foot wouldn't hold my weight, but amazingly there was absolutely no pain. No tendon tear. No damage. It was fully healed. Through prayer, in the name of Jesus.

A couple of years ago I was talking with another leader in our church about how we might balance our church budget for the coming year. We'd been wrestling with the figures for many weeks, because there were things we felt the Lord was asking of us that would stretch us financially – and we weren't convinced that we could rely on increased giving to cover it all. So we prayed and asked the Lord to give us the money we needed. Later that very afternoon Melissa, our church finance manager, received an email saying we were to receive a large gift from a legacy received by a church member that would more than cover the increase we needed. She told us straight away, and we were overjoyed. The timing of the gift was incredible, as it felt like our prayer had been immediately answered!

Others prayers take longer to be answered. Sam and I visit monthly a wonderful woman in our church who has multiple sclerosis (MS). We've been doing that now for about four years. As we've prayed, God has done some lovely things, and the MS has not developed as fast as anticipated, but she's not yet healed, despite our regular and persistent praying. But we won't give up, because Jesus said that disciples 'should always pray and not give up'.[10]

Sam and I have been praying for years that our family members who do not yet know Christ will start to follow him. We are still waiting for some of these prayers to be answered. The fact that we don't see immediate change doesn't mean we give up. We've learned that we simply need to persevere, and so we keep praying.

If we want to see our lives, and the lives of people in our communities, changed and impacted with the good news of Jesus, we need to pray, and keep praying. Martin Luther knew this, saying, 'If I should neglect prayer but a single day, I should lose a great deal of the fire of faith.'[11] It's also true that prayer doesn't just change us; it also changes the things for which we pray. I truly believe that nothing of lasting significance happens without prayer. That's why the ministry of communities like the many Houses of Prayer across the UK is so important – in fact, much more significant than most people realise. Their persistent, faithful praying is bringing God's kingdom.

We have an enemy, Satan, who hates us praying.[12] It's one of the things he most wants us not to do, because he knows that prayer is transformative. It's not a coincidence that the Bible's main teaching on spiritual warfare (in Eph. 6:10–17) flows into a call to pray (Eph. 6:18–20). The two are linked. Prayer is a form of spiritual warfare. It's likely that the church in Antioch knew this, spurring them on to be a praying church.

The one consistent emphasis I have sought to bring to the churches I've led over the last few years relates to the significance of prayer. Because prayer *is* significant. In fact, it's basic. It's what we do to get to know God better and to see his kingdom come. It's why I've written a whole book on the subject.[13] And yet many churches and many believers in Christ, especially in the West, spend little time in prayer. As God pours out his Spirit in our day, one thing he longs to do is renew our prayer life. Prayer is a sign of needing God and of our total reliance on him. If we could be a church of overflow without God's help, then there'd be no need to pray. But we can't! The work of overflow is his. We are his servants and channels of his grace. We are therefore totally dependent on him. That's why we need to pray. That's why we need churches who will pray. Like the overflowing church of Antioch.

The power of fasting

The overflowing church in Antioch not only worshipped and prayed, but they also fasted.

Fasting is the voluntary giving up of food, in order to pray.[14] Fasting is one of the basic spiritual disciplines highlighted in the Bible. It's not an optional extra for mature believers, but something every follower of Jesus, and every Christian church should practise.[15] That's why it's not surprising to see it happening in the church in Antioch. Fasting is foundational and important, releasing spiritual power well beyond the human effort put in. It's possible that the Antioch church would never have become a church of overflow if it had not been a church which fasted.

Fasting is powerful. Jesus taught that some powers of darkness are only broken through fasting.[16] Many characters in the Bible fasted,[17] and as I explain in my book, *A–Z of Discipleship:*

> **Jesus taught that some powers of darkness are only broken through fasting.**

> In the Bible we see people fasting . . . for a number of reasons, including: as a sign of humility; a sign of repentance; a sign of grief; when seeking protection; when seeking guidance; when seeking healing; when choosing leaders; in preparation for spiritual warfare; to avert national disaster; for general spiritual growth.[18]

When we fast, we voluntarily deny our body food. We then channel our hunger for food into hunger for God. We cry out to him and wait for him. While it's good to fast as part of a weekly rhythm of prayer and discipline, sometimes we fast for a purpose. At The Belfrey we've been learning about this in recent years. As I write this, we're about to enter into three days of prayer and fasting, intentionally fasting for the purpose of seeking greater overflow. Some will fast from food altogether and just drink water. Others will fast from one meal each day.[19] The time spent on these things will then be spent in prayer. Fasting helps us. It helps us to develop self-control. It helps us to identify with the poor. It helps us to turn our hunger for food into hunger for God. It helps us to become more sensitive to the Holy Spirit. And it helps us to pray. It spurs us to pray. And empowers us to pray. That's why Mark Batterson is right when he says that 'an empty stomach may be the most power-ful prayer posture in Scripture'.[20]

Churches that seek to be communities of overflow need to fast. Most churches in the West for many years have forgotten to practise this ancient but basic discipline.[21] It's thrilling to see churches beginning to learn to fast again. Such churches are likely to be overflowing churches.

The overflow of worship, prayer and fasting

People who worship, pray and fast tend to be people of over-flow. They are normally people who positively influence oth-ers. As they do these things, so God hears them, speaks to them and uses them.

A great example in the Bible of such a person is found in Luke 2:36–38 in a woman called Anna. Here's what we're told about Anna, who met Mary and Joseph when they vis-ited the temple in Jerusalem with the baby Jesus, soon after his birth:

There was . . . a prophet, Anna, the daughter of Penuel, of the tribe of Asher. She was very old; she had lived with her husband seven years after her marriage, and then was a widow until she was eighty-four. She never left the temple but worshipped night and day, fasting and praying. Coming up to them at that very moment, she gave thanks to God and spoke about the child to all who were looking forward to the redemption of Jerusalem (vv. 36–38).

Anna was a woman dedicated to worship – all the time: 24/7. This doesn't mean that she never slept. It just means that in everything she did, her mind and heart were directed to God. When you meet people like this, there's something beautiful and lovely about them. Their waking and sleeping thoughts are for the Lord.

Anna was also a person of prayer. Calling out to God. Interceding. Asking. She'd been doing it for years and it was natural to her. Would that there were more such prayer warriors in our day.

Anna also fasted. We're not told when or how often. But it was not just something she did every now and then, but it was part of the rhythm of her life. No doubt she did this because she knew that power was released through fasting.

This woman, Anna, was 'a prophet'. That means she heard from the Lord and shared his messages. She wasn't a prophet on a national scale, as there'd been no national prophet for nearly four hundred years and none would appear until John the Baptist, about thirty years later. So she probably prophesied on a more local and personal level, praying for people and sharing prophetic messages with them as she worshipped in the temple. This is what she did with Mary and Joseph, sensing that in Jesus they had a most special baby – indeed, the one who would 'redeem' and set people free. It's notable that her ministry as a prophet functioned well in the context of worship, prayer and fasting. We've found this to be the case in York. Prophecy thrives in the context of worship, prayer and fasting. These three practices support the prophetic culture explored further in Chapter 5, helping produce overflow.

This was exactly what the Antioch church discovered too. It was in the context of their worship, prayer and fasting that prophetic words came. It was such a prophetic word that sent out Barnabas and Saul on mission – on what is now commonly known as Paul's First Missionary Journey.[22] This is the first of three missionary journeys that led to the evangelisation of that region, the planting of churches and ultimately the spread of the church worldwide. It came from Antioch. Out of a community who loved to worship, pray and fast.

Also, when Saul and Barnabas established new churches in the communities they visited, Luke gives us fascinating insight into their practice:

> Paul and Barnabas appointed elders for them in each church and, with prayer and fasting, committed them to the Lord, in whom they had put their trust.[23]

So they continued to pray and fast. And they modelled this to the new believers in every community to which they were sent. Prayer and fasting, in the context of worship, creates a healthy and open atmosphere for the Holy Spirit to speak, work and equip, creating churches of overflow.

The world today needs churches that are full to overflowing with God's Spirit. It needs them to be spilling out to influence their region. This will happen as churches keep things simple and practise the basic disciplines of worship, prayer and fasting.

Application: Valuing worship, prayer and fasting

Questions for disciples and church leaders to consider from this chapter:

1. Do you love to worship? How are you encouraging your church to prioritise the worship of God?

2. How important is prayer to you? Are you modelling a prayerful life to your church? Do you encourage your church to be a praying church, and regularly share stories of answered prayer?

3. Do you experience the power of fasting in your life? Does your church fast? If not, why not?

4. Which of these three disciplines does your church need to focus on in the coming days?

5. Are you asking the Lord to pour out his Spirit of 'power, love and self-discipline' (2 Tim. 1:7) on you, so that you can mature in these disciplines?

Giving Away

Over the years, I've watched the ministry of the London church Holy Trinity Brompton (HTB) grow and expand, and it's been wonderful to see. They've planted many churches in London and beyond. They're a great example of an overflowing church. One of the main reasons for this is because they have faithfully and obediently given away. John Wimber, who started the Vineyard movement, highly influenced HTB in the 1980s and 90s, teaching that gifts are for giving away.[1] I've watched HTB, under the faithful leadership of Sandy Millar and Nicky Gumbel, apply that principle whenever they can and as they've done that, so the Lord has blessed them and multiplied their work.[2]

That's what happens when we give away. God gives more, so we can give again. Jesus taught this, and the Bible teaches this time after time.

There is a strand in the church which misuses this biblical teaching on giving, seeing its end as personal gain. The motivation for giving is therefore not about helping others but rather helping yourself. This so-called *prosperity gospel* teaches that we give in order to be blessed and get more for ourselves, which is not the main point of giving at all! If anything, that's a selfish gospel, driven by greed. While God, of course, is a good Father and wants to reward us[3] and for us to enjoy what he gives, the main reason God gives back to us is not so we hold on to what he's given, but rather that we can continue to be generous and give away again. We give away to help others. To influence others. To see his kingdom extend and increase. We give away for the purpose of overflow.

Giving away that leads to overflow

The church in Antioch understood this, probably because Barnabas modelled it to them. Maybe he talked about his experience in the early days of the church in Jerusalem when he was a new believer. In those days, according to Acts 4:

> there were no needy persons among them. For from time to time those who owned land or houses sold them, brought the money from the sales and put it at the apostles' feet, and it was distributed to anyone who had need. Joseph, a Levite from Cyprus, who the apostles called Barnabas (which means 'son of encouragement'), sold a field he owned and brought the money and put it at the apostles' feet (vv. 34–37).

Now, some years later, Barnabas finds himself leading the church in Antioch, and Agabus prophesies to the Antioch church that there is going to be a famine across the entire Roman world. This would have included their city and region. Rather than deciding to hoard food or save money for this situation for themselves, their response was to give. To give away, generously and freely. We're told:

> The disciples, as each one was able, decided to provide help for the brothers and sisters living in Judea. This they did, sending their gift to the elders by Barnabas and Saul (Acts 11:29–30).

In giving like this they were fulfilling the teachings of their Master, Jesus Christ, who said that if we give generously like this, God will pour in again, so we can give again. In Luke 6:38 he expresses it like this:

> Give and it will be given to you. A good measure, pressed down, shaken together and running over, will be poured into your lap. For the measure you use, it will be measured to you.

This teaching of Jesus tells us at least four foundational things about giving away, which can be applied to all kinds of giving.

First, *we need to give away*. It's what disciples are called to do. In fact, it's a command. Jesus said, 'Give'. Giving is not an optional extra for disciples. It's part of Discipleship 101. When Jesus teaches in Matthew 6 about basic disciplines he doesn't say '*if* you give' but '*when* you give'.[4]

Second, *as we give away, God gives to us again*. He loves to respond to our giving. This is good news, and reassures us that the Lord understands that there is a cost to giving and that he will take care of us.

Third, *God gives generously*. Not only does he give a 'good measure' but as the God of overflow he gives so that it is 'running over'. Brian Houston is therefore right when he says that 'overflow . . . is about abundance'.[5] This is his nature – to give

41

abundantly and generously. He loves to give. He gives his very self to us, which is beautifully described in The Passion Translation of Psalm 23:5: 'you give me all I can drink of you until my heart overflows.' The ultimate expression of this is seen in God giving us his best gift of all, his Son, and sending him into the world to live, die, rise and ascend to give us eternal life.[6] And as the God of overflow he continues to give generously, day by day. This is *very* good news! He's the God of too much. This is so we can give again.

Fourth, *the more generous we are, the more generous God is.* This is not favouritism. This is wisdom.[7] It is the Lord wisely choosing to invest well. He has vast resources and is looking for good places to invest those resources. When he finds a person or family or church using his resources wisely, he's pleased to give again, knowing he'll get a good return for his investment.

Jesus taught this in a number of his parable-stories, including the parable of the bags of gold (in Matthew 25:14–30), where three servants were given bags of gold while their Master was away – one received five, another two and another received one. On their return the Master found that the one with five had turned his into ten. The one with two now had four, but the servant with just the one had done nothing with his. In response the Master takes the one bag from the servant who did nothing and gives it to the one with ten. Why? Because in God's kingdom 'whoever has will be given more, and they will have an abundance' (v. 29).

God is looking for a good return for his investment. Investment bankers know the only way for money to grow is not to keep hold of it but to be brave and use it, by investing in various projects. This involves risk – it's a step of faith. You have to invest it somewhere. Jesus taught that his disciples need to do the same with all that God gives, by investing in people and in kingdom projects. When disciples give away like this, so the Lord gives back in abundance, so they can give away again. Such is the economy of the kingdom of God.

Sam and I discovered this on my occasions. One of the first times was early in our marriage when we'd saved up for a new television for our home. Just as we were about to spend the money and buy one, our church had a gift day. We had no other spare money and we felt the Lord prompt us to give the money we'd saved up for the TV. We did this, and within two weeks we'd been given an unexpected gift which was more than we needed for the television. Such is the kindness and generosity of the Lord, giving back, and motivating us to give again.

So, overflow comes as we give away. This teaching on giving away can be applied in a variety of ways, including not just giving away of money but also, for example, in the giving away of love.

Giving away love

Showing love, through kindness and care, is supposed to be central to the lives of Christ-followers. Giving like this is good and changes the world.

Most of us know that we don't run out of love. There's always more. Why? Because God gives generously to those who give like this. This is why Paul says in 1 Thessalonians 3:12, 'May the Lord make your love increase and overflow for each other and for everyone else, just as ours does for you.' God's love overflows, so that the more love we give, the better we get at giving it away. Love grows.

Some churches are very good at growing ministries of love. They seem to have a good number of projects that work with the vulnerable, the broken and the hurting. In our region I see some of the wonderful work coming out of Life Church, a great example of an overflowing church in Bradford, West Yorkshire. I'm thrilled by how God uses this church to show love in such practical ways. What most people fail to realise is that this work at Life Church and in similar places began small, often inspired in the first instance by just a few people whose hearts were touched by the Holy Spirit to do something to show practical love to people in need. From that one ministry of love, so more grew. As we give love, God gives more, so we can give again. Love begets love.

Giving away time

Overflow through giving away also occurs through the giving of time.

Time is one of our most valuable resources. As we prioritise our relationships, so the Lord ensures that we have more than enough time to give to those he's put

> We do have time. More than enough.

around us. I find it fascinating that while we easily believe we have enough love to give away, we don't think the same about time. Maybe that's because most people in the West have had instilled into them from childhood that there's never enough time. By school-age most of us have heard many thousands of times the words: 'We don't have time!' The result is that we believe it, resulting in us rushing around or failing to stop for those God puts in front of us. But God's view of time is very different to ours.[8] We do have time. More than enough.[9]

This is perhaps seen most clearly in the biblical notion of the sabbath, where God's people are called to take a full day of rest at the beginning of each week. Genesis 2 shows us that after making human beings, the very next thing God did was rest.[10] This modelled to humanity that we work from a place of rest, rather than rest from work.[11] It's fascinating to see that many today are realising that resting well is central to working well.[12] God promises that if we take a weekly day of rest, prioritising corporate worship and making space for family and community, then it will do us good, and also there will be ample time in the other six days to do everything we're called to do.[13] So resting is not about dutifully and reluctantly deciding not to work; rather it's about learning to value rest and trusting that there is more than enough time in the rest of the week to do everything that's needed.

To be honest, I used not to believe this, and still struggle, but the Lord is beginning to change my mind on the gift of time. I used to think that there is *so* much to do and *so* little time. I sought to apply all the best theory on time management – and some of that is helpful, as it's good to act efficiently and not waste time. But now I'm starting to learn to be led by the Holy Spirit and listen more attentively to his guidance. Last year, for example, I felt the Lord nudge me to spend time with a man who caught my attention. The result was that I was an hour late for a meeting, but I didn't mind, as by the end the man had given his life to Jesus Christ and been filled with the Holy Spirit! He's now joined our church. Partly because the Lord has been changing my mind about the giving of time.[14] As this happens, I know the Spirit wants to lead me to use my time well, and better. And he's telling me not to believe the lie that there isn't enough time. This is starting to change the way I live and work and rest. (But I know I still have some way to go!)

Giving away money

Overflow also comes as we give financially. In fact, I believe that giving away money is, for most of us, the main way that God teaches us about the economy of his kingdom and how overflow comes.

For many, money is one of the hardest things to let go. John Wesley, the founder of the Methodist movement used to say that following Jesus was a process of conversion, beginning with the conversion of the heart to Christ, and that 'the last part of a man to be converted is his wallet'.[15] Wesley understood that we often hold on tightly to our money. But Jesus said that there is great blessing in giving away our money. In giving it generously and sacrificially.[16] If we do this, God will look after us,[17] so we not only survive but thrive and can give away again. The only way to see if this is true is to do it, and to start giving away money.

The Bible teaches that disciples should give tithes and offerings at their place of worship.[18] That they should plan this and do this regularly.[19] This doesn't stop us also being generous more spontaneously when there is need.[20] Of course, there is a cost, but God will look after us as we do this.

Sam and I have done this for all our married life. We believe that all resources come from God and that at least the first 10 per cent of our income is his without any need for further asking, and goes to the local church. As we've done this, the Lord has never let us down, so we now give more than a tithe to church and we pray that we're able to give away more money each year than the year before. On top of this, we support other good causes, including the education of various children overseas and the work of a few chosen charities and individuals.

We've also had people come to live with us from time to time who are in need, and absorbed the cost of this. The Lord continues to teach us about the giving of our finances, proving time and again that he loves to respond to generous giving.

I've met countless people who've found the initial giving of money very difficult, fearing they will not have enough. However, once they start giving generously, they are surprised to find that God looks after them. That's what Jesus said would happen. He taught that as disciples give, they will always have more than enough. So they can give again.

The clearest teaching in the Bible on this kind of giving away of money is found in 2 Corinthians 9, which says:

Remember this: whoever sows sparingly will also reap sparingly, and whoever sows generously will also reap generously. Each of you should give what you have decided in your heart to give, not reluctantly or under compulsion, for God loves a cheerful giver. And God is able to bless you abundantly, so that in all things at all times, having all that you need, you will abound in every good work. As it is written:

'They have freely scattered their gifts to the poor;
their righteousness endures for ever.'

Now he who supplies seed to the sower and bread for food will also supply and increase your store of seed and will engage the harvest of your righteousness. You will be enriched in every way so that you can be generous on every occasion, and through us your generosity will result in thanksgiving to God (vv. 6–11).

Each of these six verses shows us something important about giving money.

First (v. 6), *we reap what we sow*. That's why it's good to be as generous as possible with our financial giving. It benefits not just the recipient but also the giver! The teachings of Jesus in the Gospels and the

> It's good to be as generous as possible with our financial giving.

rest of Scripture are patently clear on this, with Galatians 6:7,8 saying, 'A man reaps what he sows. Whoever sows to please the flesh, from the flesh will reap destruction; whoever sows to please the Spirit, from the Spirit will reap eternal life. Let us not become weary of doing good.'

Second (v. 7), *we're not to give begrudgingly*. Don't give just because the Bible tells you to. Instead, test your heart, to ensure that you're giving freely and with the motive of helping. 1 Corinthians 13:3 says I might give everything I own to the poor but unless my motive is love, then 'I gain nothing'.

Third (v. 8), *as we give our money, the Lord will ensure that we have all we need,* so we can do all the good work he's called us to. We will always have more than enough. Peter discovered this when he first met Jesus and was encouraged to go out fishing again. The catch he brought in was enormous,[21] showing him not only that he was called to a work of significant impact but also, practically speaking, that God would look after him and always provide him with more than enough. I have always found this to be true, as have the churches in which I've served and worshipped over the years: in St James's in Doncaster (1990–93); in St Aldate's in Oxford (1993–96); in Christ Church Dore in Sheffield (1996–2000); in St Chad's Woodseats in Sheffield (2000–08) and in St Michael le Belfrey in York (2009-date).

Fourth (v. 9), *God especially likes it when our gifts help the poor*. The Lord has a bias to the poor[22] and to those who have little or nothing materially.[23] Disciples are called to help the

48

disadvantaged, vulnerable and weak. We've felt, in recent years at The Belfrey, a fresh call to step up our care for the poor as part and parcel of seeing God's kingdom come. Giving to the poor in this way is both a sign of overflow and also encourages greater overflow. The Bible is clear that the Lord especially looks after those who care for the poor, as they're doing something close to his heart, with Proverbs 19:17 saying, 'Whoever is kind to the poor lends to the LORD, and he will reward them for that they have done.' The poor also includes the spiritually poor – that is, those who do not yet know the love of Christ. We're also to invest in seeing them become rich in faith.

Fifth (v. 10), *the Lord wants our giving to make a difference in the world around us.* We're not just here on planet Earth to take up space but to bring transformation. The Lord wants this more and more. Which is why it's good to target financial giving to organisations or people who are making a real difference. Recently at The Belfrey, for example, we've teamed up with Tearfund[24] in supporting a project that's bringing genuine spiritual and economic transformation to one of the poorest places on the planet in Uganda. It's all part of overflow.

Sixth (v. 11), behind all this is God's desire that we might not just be generous sometimes, but *be a people characterised by a generous lifestyle.* This will result in thanksgiving to God and will help his mission in the world. Our generous financial giving has many benefits. It's all part of overflow. I saw this modelled most clearly in 2017 when I visited Rwanda with a Tearfund team led by Nadine Parkinson. There I saw a kind of kingdom transformation that I had never seen before. In a nation where so many are economically poor, I met person after person who had found faith in Christ and was being lifted out of poverty. How was it happening? It was happening as disciples in that nation were beginning to see, through reading the Bible and applying it very practically, that God had already given them everything they needed to live and thrive, both spiritually and economically. They were learning to invest their little and see it multiply. They were learning to give to church, and to neighbours in need. This involves a world view change, from a mindset of poverty and dependency to a mindset of plenty and generosity. All this was summed up for me so beautifully in a conversation I had with one of the Anglican bishops who, when I asked him what the Lord was saying to them, said, 'God is showing us that we are rich. That we have all we need.' I was stunned by this answer, from someone leading a church in a land that, to people in the West, is extremely poor. I knew his word was true and prophetic and if he could get his church to believe it, their region and nation would certainly be transformed.

Giving away, however, is not just about giving our love and time and money. Or about giving to the poor. It's also about giving away *people*. This is an often overlooked but crucial aspect of giving away.

Giving away people

The church, as we noted in the Introduction, is about people. It's about people who are loved and saved by God, who pray and work to see God's kingdom come here on earth as in heaven.[25] People are one of the greatest resources that the church has, and so, like any other God-given resource, people are supposed to be given away too. We're not to hold on tightly to them, as often God asks us to give them away, and often the best and most gifted ones. It's all part of overflow.

The church of overflow in Antioch soon discovered this. We noted above that when they wanted to send their financial gift to the believers in Judea, they sent it with their two most gifted leaders.[26] That meant that these leaders were away for a while. The believers in Antioch were not overly concerned about this. They didn't fear the church would fall apart while they were gone! Instead, they trusted that God would look after them. And it was also an opportunity for others to lead.

> We're in real danger if we become too possessive and territorial about the Lord's resources.

Later, as we read in Acts 13, a prophetic word made it clear that God was calling Barnabas and Saul to go again, on what's now known as Paul's First Missionary Journey. Did the Antioch church resent giving them away again? No! They happily let them go in order to see God's kingdom advance. We're told (in Acts 13:3), 'So after they had fasted and prayed, they placed their hands on them and sent them off.'

This tells us that the Antioch church was willing to give away people. Often their best people. Overflowing churches understand this, and trust that the Lord will make up for the loss.

At The Belfrey, we've given away all sorts of great people over the years. As a city-centre church, people travel in to join us and become part of our community. Sometimes after a while some feel the Lord call them to join their local churches to help strengthen them. Over the years we have sent leaders and people to intentionally revitalise a church or start a new one. We're aiming to do more of this in the coming years (see Chapter 8). Others have gone to be trained for ordination and to lead other churches, especially in the north. This giving away of people is all part of overflow.

When people leave us there's always an initial gap. There's an *emotional gap*, where we miss their presence, their love and their friendship. This is natural and understandable. There is also a *physical gap*. When a family is sent out, they no longer take up a particular row in church or sofa space at the small group meeting. There is a *skills gap*, where we miss their gifts and talents. There is a *financial gap*, with their tithes and offerings now going elsewhere. And then there's the *spiritual gap* they leave as they're no longer present to pray, to care, to lead or be around. So, giving people away creates all sorts of gaps. Leaders need to be aware of this, as some people especially struggle. They find such gaps profoundly uncomfortable. But God knows that sending people out inevitably creates space, which he will fill, in time. Leaders have an important job in reassuring their people that God is in this, and all will be OK!

Gaps aren't all bad, because gaps create space. Space for others to inhabit. This is especially true of leadership. Others have to step up and lead. Sometimes people are surprised to find that they have the ability to lead, and with some coaching and guidance, can do this well. We're beginning to see at The Belfrey that it helps if you can create some kind of leadership pipeline, so that the next phase of leadership is ready. We have much to learn about this, and are aware that others are doing this much better than us, but get this right and the potential for giving away and for overflow accelerates.

When the church in Antioch gave away Barnabas and Saul – sending them to Jerusalem, and then on their missionary journey – I suspect they actually realised that they weren't really theirs to give in the first place! People, including leaders, are gifts from God and ultimately belong to him. They are with us for a while but the Lord is free to move them around as he sees fit in order to advance the kingdom of God. The same is true of all God's resources, including money. In giving us the kingdom, the Lord gives us these kingdom resources,[27] but we're called to hold them lightly. We're in real danger if we become too possessive and territorial about the Lord's resources. Instead we're called to be trustworthy 'stewards' of God's resources,[28] including his very presence.[29] This also includes stewarding the planet,[30] people,[31] property,[32] gifts[33] and money.[34] As we grow in our understanding of what it is to be stewards, so we see that it's all part and parcel of being people who give away.

The church of overflow in Antioch did this time and time again. They sent out Barnabas and Saul to Jerusalem and then on the First Missionary Journey, later sending out Paul on his Second Missionary Journey (in Acts 15:36ff) and then on his Third (in Acts 18:23ff). To do this was to obey God's call – both for the people going and for the Antioch church. They were called to be a missional church, overflowing with grace and sending out excellent people to serve God's mission in the region and beyond.

So, giving away is at the heart of overflow. A church of overflow knows this – that God is a giving God. 'In the beginning' he took a world that was initially 'empty'[35] and began to fill it up with good gifts of his creation. Despite humanity's sin and many failures, he continued to speak, to protect and to guide, wanting to abundantly provide for his people.[36] At the cross, he gave away his very best in giving Jesus Christ, releasing immense grace into the world and into our lives.[37] Today he continues to pour out his Spirit.[38] And he gives us all the resources of heaven we need, to do what he has called us to do.[39] In response, we too are called to overflow and give away. It's part of a beautiful divine partnership into which we're invited. As we give away, so God gives more so we can keep giving. But if we stop giving away, we stop the overflow, because there's no overflow without giving away.

For church communities to really 'get' all this and embrace it, it needs to be taught and modelled by leaders. In fact, leadership is crucial in all churches, and especially in churches committed to overflow. So in Part Two we will examine the kind of leaders we see in the church in Antioch – leaders who helped facilitate overflow.

As I've read and reread the story of Antioch multiple times in the context of the missional expansion of the church described in the Acts of the Apostles, and sought to examine the Antioch church in the light of the rest of the New Testament, I've come to the conclusion that we see in Antioch five key leadership roles. Luke especially highlights two of these – prophets and teachers – when he comments on the leadership in Antioch.[40] However, on closer examination I believe we see in Antioch all five of the roles described by Paul in Ephesians 4:11 – 'apostles, prophets, pastors, teachers and evangelists.' Two were especially dominant, but the other three were also very present. That's why the next five chapters, on leaders who facilitate overflow, explore each one of these leadership roles in turn, beginning with the pastor.

Application: Learning to give away

Questions for disciples and church leaders to consider from this chapter:

1. When was the last time you personally experienced the generosity of God in your life?

2. Have you discovered that God loves to gives back, in response to our giving?

3. Is God asking you to give extraordinary love in a particular situation at present? If so, don't be afraid to ask for his help and generous resourcing.

4. 'God gives us more than enough time.' Do you believe this? If not, ask the Lord to change your mind so that you see him giving you all the time you need.

5. Is God calling you to give away a sum of money? Is anything holding you back?

6. Church leaders often don't like to give away people, but they're actually the resource the Lord may ask us to give away. If he has asked you to give away people recently, it's OK to ask him to replenish and bring you more fantastic people. So ask!

PART TWO

LEADERSHIP FOR OVERFLOW

Joyful Community:
The gift of the pastor

A young couple in their early twenties walked into our church in York recently, a few minutes after our second morning service had ended. People were chatting to each other while drinking coffee and enjoying refreshments. Children were playing. Some people were being prayed for and there was contemporary music in the background. I noticed the couple wandering in, looking up and around and taking in the surroundings and the ambience, and so I went up to them and introduced myself.

'What is this place? And what's going on?' they asked me.

'Hi. This is a church. We've just finished one of our services here and we're having refreshments,' I replied, enquiring whether they'd like coffee.

They then asked lots of questions. About the church. The music. What people were doing. About what was happening as they saw people laying hands on each other as they prayed.

I told them about Jesus and his presence and how we loved to worship him and pray to him. After a few minutes the conversation ended with the young man saying, 'I love the feel of the atmosphere in here. It feels warm. Good. Positive.'

I think he was trying to tell me that he felt 'joy' in our church. He didn't actually use the word, but when he left and I reflected on our conversation, the word 'joy' was very much on my mind. Because the presence of joy is both lovely and attractive.

The Antioch church was a particularly joyful community. I am convinced of it. In the same way that the young man never used the word 'joy' in our conversation, neither does Luke – the writer of Acts – use the word in his description of the Antioch church. However, read between the lines and you see a church in Antioch that's vibrant, positive and lively. It's a community of people who are pleased to follow Jesus. They're a church that loves to encourage and tell stories. They're amazed by Christ, love worshipping and praying to him and are thrilled to tell others about him. This church is a joyful people.

'Joyful' is a better word than 'happy'. While it might be partly right to describe the Antioch church as 'happy', it's more theologically accurate to use the word 'joyful' because happiness is an emotion – a feeling which comes and goes – whereas joy is a state of being that's not dependent on changing circumstances. Paul describes this state of being in Philippians 4:11–13, saying:

I have learned to be content whatever the circumstances. I know what it is to be in need, and I know what it is to have plenty. I have learned the secret of being content in any and every situation, whether well fed or hungry, whether living in plenty or in want. I can do all this through him who strengthens me.

It is, of course, the Lord who strengthens him, with his joy. Joy was a virtue of Jesus. The letter to the Hebrews describes

Jesus as having been 'anointed' by God the Father 'with the oil of joy'.[1] It is this joy that strengthened Jesus and does the same for us. That's what joy does. It provides a robustly cheerful and contented inner resilience, which is why Nehemiah in the Old Testament famously and rightly told his people that 'the joy of the Lord is your strength'.[2]

Many secular authors agree with this distinction between happiness and joy. Richard Sheridan, author of *Joy, Inc.,* a fascinating book about joyful businesses, helpfully explains the difference:

> There is nothing wrong with happiness, and there is no question you should also seek happiness. It's just that joy is deeper, more meaningful, and purposeful. Happiness is more a momentary state of being. You can be joyful without being happy every moment.[3]

The source of joy

The Bible shows that joy is placed in the hearts of believers as they come to know Christ.[4] As the saying goes: know Christ, know joy.[5] Some, like Dwight L. Moody, experience this joy and its corresponding emotion of happiness in an encounter with the Spirit of Christ. In R.A. Torrey's account of Moody's life, he writes:

> on his way to England, he was walking up Wall Street in New York . . . and in the midst of the bustle and hurry of that city his prayer [for encounter] was answered; the power of God fell upon him as he walked up the street and he had to hurry to the

house of a friend to ask that he might have a room by himself, and in that room he stayed alone for hours; and the Holy Ghost came upon him, filling his soul with such joy that at last he had to ask God to withhold His hand, lest he die on the spot from very joy.[6]

This joy was no doubt discovered by the believers in Antioch as they became followers of Jesus. It would have overflowed in their worship and prayer and witness, and stirred the attention of those around them. Maybe it's one reason why the church grew rapidly in phases two and three (AD42–45).

Joy is supposed to be a characteristic of every believer and every church. The Bible says so, with Galatians 5:22 describing joy as one of the fruit of the Holy Spirit. If we 'live by the Spirit' (Gal. 5:16) and are 'led by the Spirit' (Gal. 5:18) then this fruit will be present, growing and developing in us. That was the case for the church in Antioch. Joy seems to have been one of their chief characteristics. However, most people know and have experienced churches that seem far from joyful. Spend time in them and there seems little or no joy. Bethel Church leader Bill Johnson gives this helpful advice to leaders who see a lack of joy in their people:

Whenever [joy] is waning, I tell our people to find where they left their joy. Following Jesus must remain a life of joy. Joy, fully realized, has a profound effect on how people live. As a result, it impacts the sustainability of all revivals. Without joy, revivals end up falling short of becoming awakenings; therefore they never develop into God's ultimate goal – reformation. When church leadership chokes the joy out of the move of God, their wrong control also kills liberty and freedom, which are the true evidences that God is present and is doing as he pleases.[7]

Johnson's advice is crucial and also shows the importance of leadership in encouraging and sustaining joy. It's likely that in Antioch this has everything to do with Barnabas, one of its most influential early leaders.

Encouraging a joyful community

Leaders play a crucial role in setting the culture of a church. Leaders have the ability to create, change and sustain the culture of the community they lead. It's one of their crucial functions. Leadership analyst Sam Chand says that 'Culture is about relationships, communication and shared values'[8] – and he's right. As leaders live and work closely with their people, communicate clearly and model the value of joy, so joy is encouraged and grows. Barnabas was good at this, because he was an encourager.

Jesus was the greatest encourager. As followers of Jesus model themselves on their Master, so disciples are supposed to be people who encourage others, although

> Jesus was the greatest encourager.

some are especially gifted at it, and Barnabas was one of these people. We know this because he'd been given the nickname 'Son of Encouragement'. Clearly his friends saw him as an encourager! But not only that, he modelled this encouragement through his words and actions. So, one of the first references to him in the church in Antioch says that on arriving there he 'encouraged them all'.[9] It seems he couldn't help but encourage. It came naturally to him. As he encouraged his people, joy grew, for joy thrives in a culture of encouragement.

In my book *A–Z of Discipleship* there's a whole chapter on encouragement ('E is for Encourage'). In that chapter I say this:

> We live in a world with much discouragement and disappointment. So much of the news is bad news and quite often depressing. Often the stories people like to tell are negative stories, criticizing their boss, the next-door neighbour, the football team or the government. If we join in with these negative stories we become part of the problem. We become discouragers. And followers of Jesus are not immune to this. We can so easily embrace the negativity that's in much of our culture and translate it into our lives, our workplaces, our families and churches. But disciples are called to something different. To encourage. To build up. To speak well. To praise. To affirm. To be positive. We need to do this in every area of life, creating a culture of honour in our homes and churches. Instead of being cynical, sceptical and pessimistic, disciples are called to honour one another, encouraging children, friends, work colleagues, church and political leaders, and everyone we come into contact with. That's why the Bible says, 'Encourage one another and build each other up.'[10]

No one has more potential to influence and encourage a church than its leaders.[11] Indeed, churches tend to take on the character of their leaders, so that the longer the leader is there, the more it becomes like them. That's why it's crucial for church leaders to model encouragement, not just when things are going well but in the tough times, because it's then that we need encouragement more than ever! That's why leaders themselves need to be resilient and know for themselves the joy of the Lord strengthening their hearts.

As we look at the way Barnabas led the church in Antioch so we see a leader leading and pastoring well. He came as an encourager and immediately encouraged the church. But there's something else he did even before he encouraged. Something that's easily missed but central to the way he led the church. He opened his eyes to see what the Lord was doing.

Leading by seeing

This is described for us in Acts 11:23, where we're told that 'when he arrived' in Antioch from Jerusalem, Barnabas spent time looking to see what God had done and was doing. He was looking for signs of the Holy Spirit at work. Listening to stories. Observing the church in action. Luke, the author of Acts, beautifully summarises this by saying that he 'saw what the grace of God had done'. This ability to 'see' is crucial to good leadership.

When we become followers of Jesus, we're given new perspective on life. We see things differently. John, the writer of the fourth Gospel, particularly understood this, which is why much of the second half of John 1 is all about seeing. Here are a few examples:

- John the Baptist, on 'seeing' Jesus (1:36) encourages his disciples to 'look'.
- Jesus tells two disciples to 'come, and you will see' (1:39).
- Jesus tells Nathanael that he knew him because he'd already 'seen' him 'while under a fig tree' (1:48).
- Jesus then tells Nathanael that he 'will see greater things' (1:50).

John clearly wants us to notice that being a follower of Jesus involves a whole new way of seeing. It's hard to follow what you can't see, so it's especially important for us to 'see' Jesus and how he's leading us. Jesus said that at conversion our spiritual eyes are opened to him and his kingdom, for 'no one can see the kingdom of God unless they are born again'.[12] The apostle Paul develops this further in his great prayer for the church in Ephesus when he prays 'that the eyes of your heart may be enlightened'[13] – which is a prayer to see even more clearly with eyes of faith. Church leaders particularly need this – to be able to see what God is doing. Heidi Baker says that 'it matters how we look at things; it matters what we carry; it matters how we see the world'.[14] Indeed Jesus himself described his approach to ministry by saying that he only did 'what he [saw] his Father doing'.[15] He's looking to see his Father at work, and then joins in.

One of the main ways that the Lord helps me to 'see' what the Father is doing is through dreams. I receive prophetic dreams quite regularly about various situations and people. Sometimes they give me understanding of what God is doing at present. Sometimes I see into the future. Sometimes they're warnings. Sometimes I'm given words of knowledge. Sometimes I see people who I need to chat to or spend time with. It's one of the ways that the Lord prophetically guides me, so I can see what or where I should be focusing. (For more on prophecy, and developing a Prophetic Culture, see Chapter 5.)

When I get really busy, or find myself immersed in too much detail, I sometimes miss what God is doing and I fail to see. Maybe that's why the very first thing Barnabas does is pause and observe. It's likely that his future ministry in Antioch and beyond was conducted in a similar manner.

Having seen what the Lord was doing – what 'the grace of God had done' – Luke says that Barnabas 'was glad' (11:23). He was joyful! What he saw thrilled his heart. And rightly so. He saw much evidence of a vibrant, growing church where 'a great number of people' had 'believed and turned to the Lord' (11:21). Every church leader longs for and wants to see that! It delighted him. He became an even more joyful leader. The church needs more joyful leaders.

This joy inside Barnabas then spilled out of him, as he encouraged the church. He could see that the work was going really well, and yet he wasn't complacent, recognising it had the potential to go a number of ways: it could continue to grow and thrive or, like any great work, it had the possibility of decline or to go off the rails. That's why Luke tells us that Barnabas 'encouraged them all to remain true to the Lord with all their hearts' (11:23). He urged them to stay faithful. To keep following. To continue doing the basics well, and to love the Lord with everything they had. I can imagine him passionately preaching and exuberantly exhorting the people! Barnabas's joyful leadership was central to the believers in Antioch being a community full of joy.

Joyful and triumphant

Joy is a quality needed in followers of Jesus today. Last Christmas morning I preached at The Belfrey in York on the theme of 'Joyful and Triumphant', picking up the phrase from the first line of the famous Christmas carol, 'O Come, All Ye Faithful'. I said that the coming of Christ changes people from being sad and defeated to joyful and triumphant. I wonder if

Barnabas had a similar message to the church in Antioch when
he arrived – encouraging them to be joyful
and triumphant in their new-found faith

> Joy has a sound
> and triumph has
> a posture.

in Jesus. One thing I said in my Christmas
sermon was that joy has a sound and triumph has a posture. Here's what I meant.

Joy has a sound. If you want to know if there's joy in your
house, stop and listen. Listen to the sounds. Listen for sounds
like praise, thanksgiving and laughter. If you hear the opposite
kind of sounds, like criticism, negativity and fear, then coun-
ter those things with the sounds of joy. Because followers of
Jesus carry joy in their hearts, we have the ability to change the
sound and bring joy.

Triumph has a posture. We see it in how people stand. In
their body language. If people are curled up in a ball or are
hanging their head in shame, it probably shows they're not living triumphant lives. The apostle Paul says we are 'more than
conquerors through him who loves us'[16] – which means that
we're on the winning team! We can hold our heads up high and
stand tall. We are not alone. Jesus, who is God with us, is near,
and by his Spirit lives in all who trust in Christ. So, we're not to
have low self-esteem, thinking we're nobody. We're loved and
precious to God. We're forgiven and set free. We've a renewed
identity that comes from faith in Jesus. And we're called confidently to pass on this faith to others and to show his love in
practical care and action. Not out of arrogance, thinking we're
better than others, but out of triumph, knowing what Christ
has done and won for us. We're joyful and triumphant because
of our faith in Jesus.

As Barnabas took up the leadership of the church in Antioch,
so he used all his gifts, skills, talents and abilities to encourage

them in their faith in Jesus. Three of his attributes are specifically mentioned in Acts 11, with Luke then saying that 'a great number of people were brought to the Lord' (11:24), suggesting that these attributes of Barnabas helped the church grow. So what were they?

Joy and goodness

The first attribute mentioned is that Barnabas 'was a good man' (11:24).

This was a simple summary of Barnabas' character. It's noteworthy that Luke mentions his character before anything else. Paul does the same in his list of leadership qualities in 1 Timothy 3. That's because our character is more important than our abilities or skills. Skills can often be developed and, where weak, can be compensated for by others, but character deficiency is much more problematic. As Rick Warren says in *The Purpose Driven Life*:

> God is far more interested in what you are than in what you do. We are human beings, not human doings. God is much more concerned about your character than your career, because you will take your character into eternity, but not your career.[17]

To be described as 'good' in first-century Greco-Roman culture was a compliment. The Greek word used by Luke is the word '*agathos*', which is an adjective used of a person or thing that is *intrinsically* good in nature, whether it is seen to be or not. So, to be described using this word for 'good' means you were habitually good – not just when people were looking!

Of course, Luke doesn't mean that Barnabas was perfect, but he does mean that he was full of moral integrity. He was consistently good in character, which I expect spilled out in kindness, love, generosity and in all sorts of practical ways.

To be good is to be like God, because one of the most simple, clear and consistent declarations throughout the Bible about the nature of God is that he is 'good'. Jesus described him not just as 'our Father' but as the 'good' Father,[18] which means he fathers us perfectly in a way that is best for us. Goodness is at the heart of his being. He is good.[19] And he does good. That's why those who love him and want to be like him should also do good. Doing good and valuing what is good is a major biblical theme and is particularly strong in Paul's short letter to Titus. In Titus the notion is used at least seven times, with the last stating that 'our people must learn to devote themselves to doing what is good' (Titus 3:14) and the first saying that leaders 'must . . . love what is good' (Titus 1:8). Leaders are supposed to exude goodness and model this to their people. Barnabas clearly did this well in Antioch.

Goodness is always expressed in practical ways. We're not told in any detail how Barnabas did this, but we can expect that his life and lifestyle displayed goodness. A contemporary example in the African church is seen in the way that leaders in the Iris movement of churches in Mozambique adopt at least two children. There are many orphan children in Mozambique, whose parents have been killed by AIDS, war or some kind of disaster. Who better to bring them up than church leaders? As they do so, showing love and care and bringing them up as their own, they also model to their churches the need to care for the weak, and the importance of loving and investing in young lives. It's just one example of church leaders today doing good.

Barnabas was pleased to do good. Goodness spilled out of him, because the good God lived within him. This goodness gave him joy and brought joy to others. Good people tend to be joyful people. Good people help create a joyful community.

Joy and the Holy Spirit

Barnabas's second attribute noted in Acts 11:24 is that he 'was full of the Holy Spirit'.

When women and men come to faith in Jesus Christ, the Holy Spirit comes to dwell within them. Indeed, you can't be a believer without having the Holy Spirit living inside you.[20] And yet not every believer is *full* of the Spirit. That's why we need to be immersed in the Spirit and be filled again and again with his presence and power.[21] This can happen spontaneously as the Spirit touches us, although normally we're filled simply by asking.[22] Our good Father loves to answer that prayer! He did so for Barnabas, who was a follower of Jesus 'full of the Holy Spirit'.

At The Belfrey, we love praying for people to be filled with the Holy Spirit. Often people sense or feel something when the Spirit of God comes upon them. Normally they feel love, and sometimes forgiveness, peace, warmth, hope and joy. Sometimes they weep, or shake, or rock, or find it hard to stand, such is the power of his presence. Others sense little or nothing, but that doesn't mean they're not being filled. Our emotions aren't always the best or only gauge of Spirit-fullness. So, how do we know when someone is full of the Spirit? Bill Johnson helpfully says that 'a bottle is not completely full until it overflows. So it is with the Holy Spirit. Fullness is measured in overflow'.[23]

So we know Barnabas was full of the Holy Spirit because of the things that flowed out of him. As well as encouragement, these would have included the fruit of the Spirit, listed in Galatians 5:22,23 (one of which – goodness – we've already noted): 'the fruit of the Spirit is love, joy, peace, forbearance, kindness, goodness, faithfulness, gentleness and self-control.'

We similarly need to make sure that these spiritual fruit are well-evidenced in our lives today, especially if we want to ensure that our churches are Spirit-filled, joyful communities. We need to teach on them, pray for them and display them inside and outside of church. These things are not just so followers of Jesus can love each other better. They're meant to flow out to those who are not yet believers in Jesus. Paul says just this in his letter to Titus, describing how 'the Holy Spirit' has been 'poured out on us generously through Jesus Christ our Saviour' (Titus 3:6) not just so we might receive 'eternal life' (Titus 3:7) but so we will be devoted 'to doing what is good' (Titus 3:8) and impact society. He's describing a church of overflow.

As we read on in the Acts of the Apostles[24] it becomes clear that the overflowing church of Antioch valued worship, prayer and fasting, which are all signs of a Spirit-filled church, as we saw in Chapter 2. We worship what we love. And we pray because we recognise our dependence on the Lord and want to develop our relationship with him. It's the Holy Spirit who stirs people to do these things and who likes to help and empower us as we worship and pray. Barnabas knew this and loved to be part of this kind of church, because he was 'full of the Holy Spirit'. Churches marked by prayer, worship and fasting are normally Spirit-filled churches. And they're churches full of joy. That was certainly the case in Antioch.

Joy, faith and testimony

A third attribute of Barnabas was that he 'was full . . . of faith'.

Faith is famously defined for us in the Bible in Hebrews 11:1: 'Faith is confidence in what we hope for and assurance about what we do not see.' It's confidently trusting in God, through Jesus Christ, both now and into the future. It has a present dimension in that Christ is with us by his Spirit – right now. That means there's an immediacy to our faith. You can, as Heidi Baker says, 'love the one in front of you'[25] and you can know at this moment God's forgiveness, presence and life-giving peace. As the Bible says, 'now is the day of salvation'.[26] But there's also a future dimension to faith which empowers us to press on with confidence, even when times are tough. We're in for the long haul and willing to stand firm and strong during periods of weakness, confusion, suffering or persecution. Ultimately, we know that we have a wonderful destiny in heaven where we'll experience God's kingdom in all its fullness. The Spirit of Jesus assures us of this, as we put our faith in Christ, and as he puts faith in our hearts.

Barnabas had this kind of faith. Indeed, he was 'full' of it! Full to overflowing.

This probably doesn't mean that Barnabas never doubted or never found following Jesus hard. It just means that he trusted God more than anyone or anything else. Bill Johnson helpfully describes faith like this: 'Faith is not the absence of doubt. It is the presence of belief.'[27] I find that really helpful and I suspect that was Barnabas's experience. One of the things that has really built my faith in recent years is hearing stories – testimonies – of God at work. It seems this was the case for Barnabas too. He loved to hear testimonies and I'm sure encouraged them in the church at Antioch.

As we've seen,[28] it was as Barnabas heard stories of changed lives and 'saw what the grace of God had done' that 'he was glad'. Later, when Barnabas returned to Antioch with Paul, after the First Missionary Journey, they told the church story after story of what God had done.[29] After that (in Acts 15, around AD50), the two of them went up to Jerusalem from Antioch to the Jerusalem Council, to help the Jerusalem church take a stance over Gentile converts. As they went, they stopped off at various churches, telling stories of what God was doing in bringing many non-Jews to faith in Christ. 'This news' we're told, 'made all the believers very glad.'[30] On arrival in Jerusalem they continued to tell these stories of faith, reporting of 'everything God had done through them'[31] which seems to have had a huge influence on the decision of the council.[32] Testimony was clearly important to Barnabas!

It's likely that Barnabas encouraged testimony in the Antioch church, because he knew that testimony builds faith. As we hear stories today of what the Lord is doing, it helps us to trust him more and believe him for the future. We've found at The Belfrey that as people share stories of what God has done in their lives, others start to believe such things can happen to them. Faith begins to rise!

I saw evidence of this recently when speaking at New Wine's 'United' summer festival on prayer. In one of the first sessions I shared a story about a woman I'd prayed for some years ago, who was healed of a sore right hip. At the end of the session, a lady approached me and said that as I shared that story she'd especially identified with the woman, as she too had a very painful hip. Not only that, but as I told the story she felt faith rise up and she knew God had touched her hip and now she was pain-free. She came to see me a few days later to tell me she was still healed. I was moved. No one had prayed for her. God just did it – as she heard the testimony!

God knows that telling stories is important and builds our faith. That's why Psalm 107:1,2 says:

Give thanks to the LORD, for he is good;
his love endures for ever.
Let the redeemed of the LORD tell their story . . .

There really is great power released in telling God-stories. As we read stories of faith in the Bible[33] and hear stories of faith today, so the Holy Spirit stirs our hearts, fills us with joy and builds our faith. Barnabas knew that a testimony-sharing, joyful church is a community of faith.

There's nothing that kills faith more than fear. Fear causes us to focus more on what others might think than on what God thinks. Fear makes us feel insufficient, insecure and ineffective. Fear paralyses us, stopping us doing what we should be doing, which is joyfully following Jesus. Fear comes from the enemy – the devil himself. He thrives on fear. Stirs fear. Longs for us to fear. The good news is that 'God has not given us a Spirit of fear, but of power, love and self-discipline'.[34] His Spirit of love – this perfect love – 'drives out fear'.[35] As the church in Antioch, under Barnabas's leadership, sought to walk in the Spirit, so fear had no place.

> There's nothing that kills faith more than fear.

I heard the church planter and author Neil Cole speak at a New Wine leadership conference a few years ago. As he did a Q&A at the end, he talked about fear and said, almost in passing: 'I think there's much fear in the UK church.' As he spoke those words, I was impacted by the Holy Spirit, sensing a strong conviction that those words were indeed prophetic words about the present state of much of the church in our nation. There is indeed much fear. Fear needs to be replaced by faith. This comes as the love of God fills us and spills out in joy. In great joy. In exceedingly great joy! The wise men who visited the infant Jesus knew something of this, as they're described in Matthew 2:10 as being 'overjoyed' – that is, having too much joy! We need to be a church so full of joy that it spills out and overflows to our family, friends and neighbours. The UK needs a faith-filled, joyful church!

This joyful church in Antioch, as we've seen, was a growing church. Barnabas encouraged its growth by being a leader full of faith. And its growth helped Barnabas continue to be full of faith. While Barnabas may not have been such a gifted evangelist as Paul, he nevertheless had a huge desire to share the good news of Jesus, and encouraged the new believers in Antioch to keep doing that, trusting that many more would find faith in Jesus. And they did! And as they did, so their joyful faith grew.

Joyful pastors

So, we've seen that Barnabas played an important role not just in encouraging numerical growth in the Antioch church, but also in shaping them into a people marked by joy. This is because he was a pastor. Pastors do this. They love people, are kind and caring and have the ability to make the people they pastor feel incredibly loved.

As we've looked at Barnabas's attributes and the way he led the church, and we then analyse this through the lens of the five-fold ministry gifts listed in Ephesians 4:11, Barnabas clearly scores high as a pastor. We see this in the way he argued with Paul about whether to take John Mark with them on Paul's Second Missionary Journey. Barnabas showed his pastoral heart in wanting to include Mark, hoping he would grow and develop.[36]

Barnabas also had good teaching gifts, as we know. Pastoring and teaching often go together, with many pastors describing themselves as 'pastor-teachers'.[37] He is also later described as an 'apostle', which is what he increasingly became as he helped establish many new churches from this apostolic base in Antioch. But in all this Barnabas never lost his pastor's heart. This was probably his 'base' or predominant ministry. It was this that helped create a joyful community in Antioch and wherever else he went.

The risk of pastors

Pastors like Barnabas are wanted in every church. Their kindness and encouragement help the church feel loved and comfortable. They like spending time with people, and they like it when people want to spend time with them. As such, pastors are often especially empathetic and feel the pain of people. All this can be very helpful, but it also has a shadow side. It's tempting for pastors, who love people and are particularly sensitive to criticism or to worry about losing people from church,[38] to tell people what they want to hear. This might, for example, include saying that a sinful lifestyle doesn't really matter, as God is full of forgiveness. Or it might involve twisting Scripture to say something it never intended to say – church history shows us that pastors are vulnerable to compromising Scripture, especially parts of the Bible that are countercultural to the society in which they are living. Such theological pragmatism is a slippery slope. It usually leads to the opposite of what pastors desire – to a loss of joy and, in the next generation, to loss of faith altogether. Luke therefore presents Barnabas as a great example of an encouraging pastor who urged the disciples in Antioch to 'remain true to the Lord' (11:23). That's why pastors need themselves to daily read God's Word, and to be listening to the teachers and prophets, in order to stay faithful to God's Word and keep their joy strong.

Joyful kingdom; joyful church

Joy is the pastor's gift. Because joy is not dependent on circumstances, a great pastor will do what Barnabas did, which is bring joy, encourage joy and want to see joy sustained in their community.

'Joy' as the scholar and author C.S. Lewis said, 'is the serious business of Heaven'.[39] In heaven we'll experience joy in all its fullness. In the meantime, between now and eternity we're to do what Jesus says, and pray that the kingdom of heaven would come here on earth.[40] This kingdom is a kingdom of joy.[41] That means we should be expecting increasing joy to be the mark of God's kingdom people today. To be honest, this is not always what I see when I look at some of the church in the UK! That's why we need to learn from Barnabas and from the Antioch church and discover what it is to be a church of overflow. They overflowed in worship and prayer and good-ness, and with the Holy Spirit and faith. They told stories of God at work, and shared their faith. This kind of community is a joyful church. A joyful church that needs pastoring well. And it's the kind of church the world desperately needs. Beni Johnson is right when she says that 'the world doesn't need our sadness; they need our joy'.[42]

Application: The gift of the pastor

Questions for disciples and church leaders to consider from this chapter:

1. To see if you might have pastoral gifts, consider the following:
   - Do I particularly identify with Bible verses like these:
     'shepherd the flock under your care' (1 Pet. 5:2)
     'rejoice with those who rejoice, mourn with those who mourn' (Rom. 12:15)
     'pay careful attention to yourselves and to all your flock' (Acts 20:28)?
     Read the three scriptures quoted above and consider what they mean.
   - Think of someone known to you who is in particular need at present. Pray for them right now. At the end of the prayer think about what the next step in pastoring them might be (e.g. go to see them; send a text, or call, or email; send a card or flowers or gift etc.). Put into practice this next step today.

2. If you think 'pastor' may be your dominant ministry:
   - Pray about this.
   - Find another pastoral person and talk with them about this.
   - Talk to your church leader about this.

3. If you are a church leader and see latent pastoral gifts in someone:

   - Ask permission to lay hands on them and pray. If they agree, pray and ask the Holy Spirit to come and release all the gifts he has for them – particularly pastoral gifts. Ask the Lord to provide, to equip and to enable.

   - Then invite the potential pastor to pray, asking the Lord to show them one person they could be caring for and encouraging at present. (Note: it should normally be a person of the same gender.) Tell them to contact that person. They may decide to meet occasionally or regularly. They should pray at least once per week for them. They are to encourage them to be growing as a follower of Jesus.

   - Agree to meet with the potential pastor again in a month, for feedback, so you can encourage them in their gifts.

Prophetic Culture:
The gift of the prophet

'Why not come over to our church next Wednesday evening?' I was asked by my friend Alex Absalom. 'We've got some prophets in town. You'd enjoy hearing from them.'

'OK,' I said, and so the following week, Sam and I went to the King's Centre in Sheffield to hear from the visiting prophets.

It was the early 2000s and between Alex's invitation and the meeting itself I'd met with a long-standing member of St Chad's, Woodseats in Sheffield – the church I was leading. I'd been at St Chad's Church for a year or so and was already starting to introduce changes that were necessary in order for us to become the kind of church God was asking of us. I had come to the church with a mandate from the church council and the bishop to bring change, and that was beginning to happen as I shared the vision of what I'd prayerfully sensed the Lord was calling us to. The chat with the church member had been memorable, to say the least. It had been more of a lecture than a conversation. I'd been informed in no uncertain terms that the plans I'd been sharing for the last year or so were not right and a few things in particular 'were never going to take place in this church'. I'd left the meeting feeling understandably deflated.

So, there I was, the following week, with Sam at the meeting with the so-called prophets. I think there were three of them. One of them began by teaching a little about prophecy from the Bible, and then said that they would demonstrate. There were probably around seventy people present and they began to call out a few people – some individuals and some couples, and one by one they shared what they sensed the Lord wanted to say to them. Some of the people were visibly moved. Then one of the prophets pointed to me and Sam.

We came out and told them we were church leaders in the city, but nothing else. Although we'd never met any of them before, one of them began to pray and talk about St Chad's Church in his prayer as if they knew us, and then he said that I was leading the church in the right direction and that the Lord was with me, but that I'd recently been discouraged by a particular conversation. In particular I'd been told that certain plans I had were never going to take place in this church. This got my attention, as he used the exact phrase that had been spoken to me the week before! The prophet then said, 'And the Lord says, that's not true. They *will* happen. Press on. Don't be discouraged.'

I was amazed by what had been shared! It was so accurate and so helpful.

Then one of them spoke over Sam.

One thing Sam had done in the church building since our arrival was try to improve a large area of wall on one side that was painted a rather nasty shade of brown. It was a big and dominant space, and Sam had the idea of pinning a large blue sheet over it and then making a display which could be changed every few weeks or so, that reflected the season we were in as a church. She'd worked with the children of the church to create two or three of these scenes so far, which not only brightened up this rather dead and dull space but also creatively communicated a message. I don't think Sam saw it as particularly significant, just an improvement to the area.

Knowing nothing about this, the prophet speaking over Sam then began to describe the current scene on the wall Sam had helped produce. He mentioned its colours and the particular layout of it, which was exactly accurate! And then he said how the Lord loved what Sam had done and that he wanted to develop and bless her artistic and creative gifts.

We were both awestruck by the accuracy of this prophetic insight. Like the message shared with me, it was a reminder that God knows and sees everything. And he wants to guide, encourage and build us up. Prophecy should do that. It certainly did for us that evening, and was so helpful in pressing on with all that the Lord was calling us to at St Chad's Church at that time. Such is the power of prophecy.

Prophecy in Antioch

Prophecy was also an important feature of the church in Antioch led by Barnabas. We know this because Luke, the writer of Acts specifically says that 'in the church in Antioch there were prophets and teachers' (Acts 13:1). These two groups of leaders played key roles in shaping the culture of this overflowing church, which is why we are exploring prophecy in this chapter, followed by teaching in the next.

In the same way that Sam and I were impacted fairly early in our ministry by some travelling prophets, so the Antioch church was also influenced and probably shaped by the ministry of visiting prophets. In phase four of the church's growth, after Saul's arrival, he and Barnabas remained in Antioch for a whole year. Luke tells us that it was 'during this time' that 'some prophets came . . . from Jerusalem to Antioch' (Acts 11:27). Barnabas welcomed and encouraged these prophets. He'd probably seen this kind of prophetic ministry in Jerusalem and he might have even met these particular prophets before.

Only one of the prophetic messages given at the time is recorded in Acts, given by a man called Agabus, although it seems there were others who shared too. The message through Agabus was about a coming 'severe famine' that 'would spread throughout the Roman world', which Luke then tells us happened later, 'during the reign of Claudius'. We're not told in what form the prophecy came (i.e. whether through a dream, vision, etc.) or how it was interpreted, but we are told how it was applied: by the church deciding to provide a financial gift 'for the brothers and sisters living in Judea' which was taken to them 'by Barnabas and Saul' (Acts 11:27–30). Clearly the church trusted these two leaders with everything – including their money.

While there's much more we'd like to know about how prophecy functioned at Antioch, we're given some insight by Luke in Acts 11:28 when we're told how Agabus prophesied, as he 'stood up and through the Spirit predicted' the famine. Three things are noteworthy.

First, he *stood up*. This was an indication, in their culture, that he had something to say of importance. While no doubt prophecy can be shared anywhere, including behind closed doors, sometimes the Lord gives words to share in a public context, which is likely here to have been during worship. That was certainly the case on another future occasion in Antioch, where an important prophetic word was given during worship. 'The Holy Spirit said, "Set apart for me Barnabas and Saul for the work to which I have called them"' (Acts 13:2). This is a reminder that when we gather for worship, we should be ready for God to speak important prophetic messages to us.

Second, he spoke *through the Spirit*. There was a recognition that what he said wasn't just good human ideas, but that he was speaking under the inspiration and guidance of the Holy Spirit. We're not told how this was discerned, but clearly they sensed that this was the Lord speaking, so much so that they responded with specific action as a church.

Third, this prophecy involved *prediction*. It foretold the future. Prophecy often does this, talking about that which is to come. However, it does not always do this. Sometimes, rather than 'foretelling' it is 'forth telling' – that is, sharing a message from God about the here and now. Whether it is about the future or the present, prophecy should encourage an individual or the church.

All prophecy should do this. It should build up. The apostle Paul says this to the Corinthian church, explaining that one purpose of prophecy is his desire that the church 'may be edified'.[1] This only happens if prophecy is affirmed. By encouraging and giving an open door to travelling prophets, Barnabas helped create and nurture a prophetic environment in his church, so much so that the Antioch church eventually became known as a prophetic church. It was a place where

> **Barnabas helped create and nurture a prophetic environment in his church.**

prophetic ministry was normative and welcomed because Barnabas had encouraged a prophetic culture.

Prophecy and a prophetic culture

A prophetic culture is an environment where prophecy is normative. In a prophetic culture prophecy is not seen as weird or wacky, but holy and helpful.

Prophecy is God communicating a message to us. It's a word in season. A message from the Lord. It can be a general message,[2] but normally it's specific – speaking directly into our lives with a message that

> Prophecy is God communicating a message to us.

resonates and is timely. Often it's personal and for individuals or a couple. But it can be more corporate in nature, being a message for a family, a small group, a church, a community, a city, or a nation.

All preaching should be prophetic, because preachers have a message from God to share from Scripture. At times, however, preaching can become strongly prophetic as the message hits home and the recipient(s) of it are touched and moved either by the whole message or a part of it. This is what happened on the Day of Pentecost when Peter preached. We're told: 'When the people heard this, they were cut to the heart and said to Peter and the other apostles, "Brothers, what shall we do?"'[3]

Prophecy does this. It pierces our hearts with a now-word from God, where we know God is speaking to us and that we need to respond. This can happen in all sorts of ways.

In August 2019, one of the female students who worships at The Belfrey and leads a small group was at a Christian festival in Peterborough. As she was worshipping, she felt the Holy Spirit speak prophetically about the man standing next to her in the tent – that he was not yet a follower of Jesus, but that he'd like to be. So, she began a conversation with him and soon found out that the message she's heard was correct. She explained the good news of Jesus and helped him say a prayer, giving his life to the Lord. She was thrilled to be used in this way! But what makes this story even more wonderful is what happened next. As they chatted further, he found out that she lived in York, where his sister lived. They then worked out that his sister worshipped at our church and was in this female student's small group! What's more, at the beginning of the academic year – some eleven months previously – they'd all shared names of people who they'd love to see start following Jesus that year. They'd written down these names on pieces of paper, and shared them out. The female student still had her piece of paper, in her Bible. And whose name was on it? The answer was – this very man! She'd been praying for him for nearly a year to start following Jesus, and then one day, 120 miles away from York she bumped into him at a festival and there, with a prophetic nudge from the Holy Spirit, led him to Christ.

I love that story, because at the heart of it is a young person wanting to be used by God, and willing to obey his prophetic voice. And look at the result!

The Lord loves to guide us so we know his direction, and he often does this through prophetic people. This has always been the case, with God telling Isaiah, 'I told you these things long ago; before they happened I announced them to you.'[4] Similarly Amos 3:7 says: 'Surely the Sovereign Lord does nothing without first revealing his plan to his servants, the prophets.' God loves to tell of his plans before he brings them about.

He is longing to pour out his Spirit of prophecy much more in our day, creating a prophetic culture in our churches.

Experts on culture and culture change tell us that it takes time for something to become embedded in a community. Even if leaders are intentional about this, it's hard to see real cultural change in less than three years.[5] That's why, if you want to see a prophetic culture develop in your church, you need to pray and preach about it as well as encourage and model it. Maybe that's one reason why Barnabas and Saul were happy for the prophets Judas and Silas to come from Jerusalem to Antioch for a time after the so-called Jerusalem Council.[6] When in Antioch these two men 'said much to encourage and strengthen the believers'. So, again we see the leaders welcoming and encouraging prophetic ministry and making it normative in their community. Here is evidence of prophetic ministry working at its best, building up the church. No wonder it was encouraged. Such is the effect of a healthy prophetic culture.

So, the Antioch church was known as a prophetic church that welcomed prophets. They practised what Jesus talked about in Matthew 10:41: 'Whoever welcomes a prophet as a prophet will receive a prophet's reward.' Commenting on this, Kris Vallotton, who heads up prophetic ministry at Bethel Church in Redding, California, says:

This indicates that the value you place on [prophecy] determines the power you receive from it . . . Grace flows from the office of the prophet. Prophets give people eyes to see and ears to hear. One of the most important functions prophets and prophetesses have in the Body of Christ is to equip each member of the Church to hear from God himself or herself, and for others in need. It is one sign of a highly dysfunctional spiritual community when the prophet or prophetesses become the main source of hearing from God. The primary responsibility of the office of the prophet and prophetess is to create a prophetic community where every member of the Body understands how to give and receive prophetic words.[7]

Creating a prophetic community is helpful for any church and especially so if the church has a vision to be a church of overflow, reaching out beyond itself and resourcing others. Equipping God's people to be prophetic and then sending them out is surely one of the best things that an overflowing church can do. That's one reason why the Bible says: 'Follow the way of love and eagerly desire gifts of the Spirit, especially prophecy.'[8]

Passionate about prophecy

Followers of Jesus are told to be passionate about spiritual gifts, particularly about prophecy. Why? Because 'the one who prophesies speaks to people for their strengthening encouraging and comfort'.[9] Most of us need to be strengthened, encouraged and comforted! And that's what happens to us when we're recipients of authentic prophetic ministry. That's why, in the same way that individuals should pursue the gift of prophecy, so it's also good and beneficial for church leaders to intentionally seek to create a prophetic culture in their church.

This is something I've been seeking to do more and more at The Belfrey in York. Whilst prophecy has been important to me for many years, I wasn't sure at first how to encourage this more widely when I arrived at The Belfrey, but the Lord has been so kind in bringing us gifted prophetic leaders in Lisa Cuellar, Kerstin Wandel and now Richard Dearden, to invest time in this and to strengthen and steer the prophetic ministry amongst us. Through various teaching courses and training days, through accountability groups and working closely with the intercessors in our House of Prayer, there's now a much greater expectation in our church community that God will speak prophetically. This can happen especially when the church meets for worship (which is the context for the prophetic gifts mentioned in 1 Corinthians 12), but also at home, at work and, in fact, anywhere! While the Holy Spirit can communicate whenever he wants, we've also been learning that the Holy Spirit loves to bring a prophetic message on special occasions – e.g. a birthday or anniversary, at New Year or the start of a new season, when we move house, when people are baptised or commissioned. There's a much greater openness amongst us now, both in general and on special occasions, to listen to the Lord. What we're learning is that if we listen, especially as we're worshipping and praying, God often speaks.

Receiving a prophetic message

A prophetic message can come at any time, although often it happens as we intentionally draw near to God in prayer. As we're talking to God, so he talks to us. It's as simple as that. As we know from other parts of the Bible, and particularly from Jesus' teaching, the Lord loves to respond to our requests,[10] so it's also good and appropriate to ask the Lord to speak prophetically. I often do this in pastoral or missional situations, in business meetings and in all sorts of contexts. I also do this before I go to sleep, as God often speaks to me in the night, and especially in dreams. It's one of the main ways I hear from the Lord. For thousands of years God has been communicating this way, with the Lord making it clear to Moses that 'When there is a prophet among you, I, the LORD, reveal myself to them in visions, I speak to them in dreams.'[11] If we want to create more of a prophetic culture in our churches, we need to encourage our people to be listening to God and expecting God to communicate. David Watson said that 'a prophet must above all learn to listen to God, discern the voice of God, and then pass on that word from God to his people'.[12]

Jesus is clear that all his followers can hear from him, saying 'My sheep hear my voice' (NRSV).[13] That's why one name given for Jesus in the Bible is 'the Word'.[14] He both embodies and brings God's message. Whereas not everyone will be a prophet, all followers of Jesus can hear him speak and can prophesy. The main way we hear from God is by reading the Bible, which has been left to us as God's Word[15] – his message to us. The Bible could, then, rightly be described as one big prophetic message to us from God. Maybe that's why Eugene Peterson called his excellent paraphrase of the Bible *The Message*. When it comes more specifically to prophetic ministry, we can be sure that no prophecy should contradict the Bible. God would not do that. This means that those seeking to be prophetic should be growing in their knowledge of the Bible and be studying it. Not only will this help ensure they don't contradict its message, but also it will help them hear from the Lord more clearly. It's as we get to know the incarnate Word – Jesus Christ, through reading the written Word – the Bible, that we can accurately share the prophetic word – through the Spirit of Jesus.

Most of the time the Spirit of Jesus communicates prophetically in creative ways, through pictures and words that require discernment. Some wish it was much simpler and matter-of-fact, but such is the nature of prophecy. As we pursue our relationship with him, so we grow in discernment. The writer of Proverbs describes it like this: 'It is the glory of God to conceal a matter; to search out a matter is the glory of kings.'[16] In explaining this and prophecy in general, Bill Johnson helpfully says: 'God doesn't conceal from you, but for you.'[17] Those adopted into his royal family must pursue him and his message. As we seek him and learn to hear from him, so we come to know him better. Communication comes out of relationship.

God sometimes communicates in an audible voice, but in my experience this is rare. I personally have only heard the voice of the Lord out loud on one occasion. It was when I was a boy and I heard the Lord call me by name three times, rather like Samuel in the Bible.[18] The only other time relates to someone who heard God's voice on my behalf – where, in two dreams, they saw and heard the Lord speaking to me in an audible voice and then they shared it with me. It was very helpful. When we receive two messages from the Lord one after the other like this, perhaps in two very similar dreams or visions, we should take this seriously as it's normally a sign of the Lord especially getting our attention and wanting to let us know that this is true and, if predictive, will happen soon.[19] We see this in the two dreams that Joseph had as a young boy[20] and in the two dreams that Pharaoh had on the same night.[21]

A number of years ago, as I was wanting to learn how to hear better from God and prophesy, I remember hearing Sandy Millar, previous vicar of HTB, say something very helpful. He said that we should practise. You should ask the Lord to speak, and then when you think you've received something prophetic, give

God the benefit of the doubt. By this he meant that so often we ask the Lord to speak and then something comes to us – maybe a thought, or a word, or an image – and we immediately think 'That can't be God!' and we discard it. But what if it was from God? After all, we've just asked him to speak! Sandy urged us to find contexts in which to practise safely. We can do this on our own, or in pairs or small groups, and in the context of prayer, have a go and share what we sense the Lord saying. As we do this, so we'll learn, over time, to hear his voice more clearly. I've sought to practise like this now for many years, and I still do. I'm getting better but still have much to learn!

As we do this, the Lord will bring things to us. When it comes to prophesying over individuals, I've found that the prophetic message I bring is rarely something the Lord has already been saying personally to me, that I pass on as a second-hand prophecy. Rather, it's more normally something that feels like it's come from left field. From out of the blue. It could come as a Scripture, or a picture. It could be a vision – which I've found is different to a picture. A picture is often still, although occasionally it develops as you see it, whilst a vision is more like watching a movie. When receiving a vision, it's quite passive – just watching and recording what you see. I've had a number of such visions, including one a few years ago the night before I was preaching in a church in Burundi. I shared the vision as part of the message I brought to the church the following day, and they found it very helpful. Dreams are rather like that too, where the recipient passively experiences the dream (after all, you're asleep!) and then, on waking records it and seeks God for its interpretation and application.

Prophetic revelation, interpretation and application

There is an important process of discernment needed with all prophecy, especially
visions and dreams, that we see clearly in
Scripture and which I have found so helpful. It's the three-fold process of revelation,
interpretation and application.[22] Sometimes people receive prophecies that are
clearly from the Lord, but they fail to go

> There is an
> important
> process of
> discernment
> needed with all
> prophecy.

through this process, with the result that the prophecy does not
have its full impact. So, going through the three-fold process is
important and helpful.

First, we receive *revelation*. This is the actual word, picture,
dream, or vision. We need to be aware of what we've received,
asking ourselves: 'What is the message?' We must be clear about
what we've seen or heard, making sure we've not missed anything. We must not add, but neither should we take away. As
well as understanding what we've received, I've also learned to
be attentive to any emotions experienced – for example, was I
pleased or happy, or troubled or fearful? These all help capture
the revelation.

One of the clearest examples of this in the Bible is found
in the two dreams of Pharaoh, in Genesis 41. The revelation
is recorded in verses 17–24, describing seven lean cows eating
seven fat cows, and also seven thin heads of corn swallowing
seven full heads of corn.

Second, we seek *interpretation*. The revelation received could
mean all sorts of things. So, we ask the Lord, 'What is the
meaning?' This is the place where it's easy to go wrong as the
revelation could have many possible interpretations. Listening

is required. So, when I wake up having received a prophetic dream, the first thing I ask the Lord is, 'What does that mean?' Sometimes I hear straight away, even whilst I'm still a little sleepy and coming round. I've learned to take what I hear then seriously, as I'm not sufficiently awake to let my own human reasoning take over! Sometimes I don't hear immediately so I then need to take time to prayerfully wait and listen.

When it came to interpreting Pharaoh's dreams of cows and corn, Joseph next gives the interpretation – in verses 25–32. He tells Pharaoh that the dreams relate to seven coming years of abundance followed by seven years of famine.

Third, we need *application*. This is sometimes missed but is nevertheless important. Here we are asking, 'What do I do?' The first and obvious thing we do with any prophetic word is pray. We pray for wisdom to know how to respond. If it involves someone else, we pray for blessing and good things for the person or situation it's referring to. If it's a message for someone else, we need to ask the Lord if we have permission to share it. The answer may be 'yes', or 'not yet', or maybe even 'no'. It might be given to you just so you can pray for them. But there's also usually a further response required. Maybe a conversation needs to be had. A phone call made. An email or letter sent. A meeting set up. Maybe something needs to start. Or stop. It could be all sorts of things. We need to ask the Lord and prayerfully listen.

In the story of Pharaoh's dreams, Joseph shares the application in verses 33–36, to which Pharaoh favourably responds and Joseph's life is changed forever.

This three-fold process can sound quite mechanical, but after a while it becomes quite normal and natural. Church leaders would do well to model this to their people. I suspect Barnabas did something like this for the church in Antioch. I've learned that it's important to write down prophecies, so I have a journal where I record all my dreams and various prophetic things that relate to my life, my family and my church. It's also great to reread these things regularly and remember what God has done (see Chapter 4).[23] Following the example of Bill Johnson, I also carry around with me a file of prophecies that have been spoken over me during my life. From time to time I get these out, thank God for his prophetic word and pray over them. On the last day of each year I reread my journals for the year. Often I'm amazed by what the Lord has done, and by getting a year's perspective I see how his prophetic word has helped and encouraged me, and very often been fulfilled. The Lord is so kind and good!

Prophetic declarations

One of the additional reasons I carry my prophecies with me is so I can declare them over myself and my context. I'm learning that there is power in declaration and that God gives authority to his church to speak into being that which has not yet happened. This is what he asked of the prophet Isaiah, saying 'Declare what is to be'[24] and he sometimes asks us to do the same. Creative power is released as we use the authority given us and declare God's prophetic word. God himself has modelled this for us in the way he created the world, declaring it into being (in Gen. 1) by saying, 'Let there be . . .' and 'there was'.

This was demonstrated quite dramatically for me a few years ago at one of our weekly staff mornings at The Belfrey. I awoke that morning with a strong urge to speak to our staff out of

Genesis 1:28 where God says to humanity, 'Be fruitful and increase in number'. So, I taught from that Scripture for a few minutes, explaining that this is God's desire for all people and that it was his particular desire for us at the time, so we should be praying for and expecting increase. At the end I asked everyone to stand so I could then declare this over the staff team. I did this for a couple of minutes and ended in prayer before we then had a coffee break. Towards the end of the coffee break one of our female interns came up to me, very excited, apologising for leaving the room when I declared Genesis 1:28 over us. She said she had to go to the WC because as I spoke that word, she'd got her period. I could tell she was thrilled, but to be honest, I wasn't quite sure why she looked so excited – and I probably looked a little flummoxed! She went on to tell me her story, that when she came to our city a few years earlier as an unbeliever she'd initially taken the contraceptive pill, but after becoming a follower of Jesus she'd come off it. However, it had affected her monthly cycle with the result that she failed to menstruate. 'But,' she said, 'when you declared "be fruitful and multiply" over us, I got my period!' I could now see why she was so excited! Her body, which had not been functioning properly, was now ready to be fruitful and multiply – and it had happened through the declaration of that word. But she wasn't just excited for herself, but for us as a church – seeing what was happening in her body as a sign showing that God really did want us to be fruitful and multiply. Such is the power of prophetic declaration!

Prophetic risk

So, prophecy is very helpful in church life – both personally and corporately, which is why it's good to develop a prophetic culture. So how come many churches don't? For some it's probably because of a lack of awareness of what prophecy is and how it works, but for others it may be the fear of risk.

Prophecy is risky. Alan Hirsch helpfully reminds us that 'because of the close association of the prophet and the unfolding of the will/heart of God, along with the innate subjectivity of this message, prophets can potentially be volatile and divisive people – especially if their gifting is immature and undeveloped'.[25] Prophecy can easily go wrong, and sometimes it does. It mustn't be overcontrolled but it does require careful stewarding. Some leaders have heard prophetic words given that have not been fulfilled, and as a result they discourage the use of prophecy, especially in public. Others become cynical and negative and question why God speaks in this way. That's why we'd do well to follow Paul's advice in 1 Thessalonians: 'Do not quench the Spirit. Do not treat prophecies with contempt, but test them all; hold on to what is good, reject every kind of evil.'[26]

Prophecy needs testing. It requires testing by the church and especially by the leadership. I have all sorts of prophetic words shared with me on a regular basis. I always try to thank people for sharing them as, with Paul,[27] I want to encourage everyone to keep eagerly desiring spiritual gifts, especially prophecy. When they are for me personally, I write them down and pray over them. Some I might discard. Ones that confirm what God is already saying particularly get my attention. When prophecies are for the church they also need to be weighed. Some I will share, some I won't. As the senior leader of the church, the final responsibility for that decision is mine. In a church meeting at The Belfrey, the decision rests with the person leading the meeting, although occasionally they may seek help from another leader around them, including me, if they're unsure. This is all part of the testing.

The other risk of prophecy is not what happens when it goes wrong, but what could happen when it goes right and prophetic people become overconfident and perhaps complacent about their gifting. When things are going well, we need to be aware of the risk of prophetic success. Every person has their weaknesses and there are particular vulnerabilities that go with particular gifts. That's why it's important that leaders not only pursue a close relationship with the Lord, but are also accountable to others. While it's something of a generalisation, I've learned that many prophetic people experience the presence and promptings of the Holy Spirit in physical ways. They often feel the Spirit of God, sometimes physically. This is good and fine and normal. It also often translates humanly into valuing touch, with physical affection often being a primary way that they feel loved.[28] All this means that prophetic people can be particularly vulnerable to sexual temptation. If you look at the history of the church, many good and gifted prophetic people have tripped up in this area, bringing prophetic ministry and the good news of Jesus into disrepute. In creating a prophetic culture, leaders need to be wise and frank about such temptations. They must put good boundaries around their ministry and take care.

Building through prophecy

Leaders therefore need to acknowledge these risks while also pursuing a prophetic culture because, at the end of the day, prophecy is really helpful, because prophecy builds. It is a building gift. Not only does it build up individuals and small groups, but it builds *the church*. That's one reason why the Bible says that the church is 'built on the foundation of the apostles and prophets'.[29] Churches are normally planted by apostolic people (see Chapter 8), sent out in response to a prophetic word. As leaders are faithful to apostolic teaching and guided by prophetic revelation, so churches grow. If you want a growing and indeed an overflowing church, you need these pioneering, building gifts that come from apostles and prophets. You also need evangelists to be working outside the church telling people about Jesus, and to sustain the church and nurture disciples you also need the evangelists inside the church telling the stories of people coming to faith and encouraging the rest of the church to be living and sharing the good news. Also, you need the pastors to be caring for the community and teachers to be faithfully teaching from the Bible. All five kinds of leaders are needed[30] – including the prophets and gifts of prophecy.

So, if we want to see old churches revitalised and new churches started in our day, we need to be a church of overflow which welcomes prophetic ministry. This was the experience of the great church of Antioch. They became known as a centre for both prophecy and teaching. That's why we now turn to the gift of the teacher.

Application: The gift of the prophet

Questions for disciples and church leaders to consider from this chapter:

1. To see if you might have prophetic gifts, consider the following:
   - Do I particularly identify with Bible verses like these:
     'eagerly desire gifts of the Spirit, especially prophecy' (1 Cor. 14:1)

     'Surely the Sovereign LORD does nothing without revealing his plan to his servants the prophets' (Amos 3:7)

     'Before I formed you in the womb I knew you, before you were born I set you apart; I appointed you as a prophet to the nations' (Jer. 1:5)?

     Read the three scriptures quoted above and consider what they mean.
   - Think of someone you know who would value God speaking to them. Pray for them right now. Then wait and see what comes. Be open to a word, picture, scripture, etc. When you sense something come (revelation), write it down, and then ask the Lord what it means (interpretation) and what you should do (application). If the Lord gives you permission, find a way to communicate this message kindly and in an encouraging manner to the person.

2. If you think 'prophet' may be your dominant ministry:
   - Pray about this.
   - Find another prophetic person and talk with them about this.
   - Talk to your church leader about this.

3. If you are a church leader and see latent prophetic gifts in someone:
   - Ask permission to lay hands on them and pray. If they agree, pray and ask the Holy Spirit to come and release all the gifts he has for them – particularly prophetic gifts. Ask the Lord to provide, to equip and to enable.
   - Then invite the potential prophet to pray, asking the Lord to show them one person with whom they can share a prophetic message. Ask them to listen. When they receive the revelation, encourage them to listen further for the interpretation and application. If they sense this is be shared with the person, encourage them to do so.
   - Agree to meet with the potential prophet again in a month, for feedback, so you can encourage them in their gifts.

Teaching Centre:
The gift of the teacher

There's been a church on or near the site of St Michael le Belfrey since the seventh century, and over the years the church has often impacted not just the city but well beyond York. So, as the leader of the church I'm part of a great heritage of saints and stand on the shoulders of giants. When asked to name significant leaders of our church most recall David Watson, who led a tremendous work of God in the 1960s to 1980s. Many discovered the love of the Father, put their faith in Christ, and experienced the presence and power of the Holy Spirit. But before David, there were others too whom the Lord used in significant ways, one of whom was William Richardson. Richardson was vicar for fifty years, from 1770 to 1820! He was known for his care for the disadvantaged, setting up the Sunday school movement in York, where many poor children were cared for and heard the good news of Jesus, and he often visited people in prison who'd got themselves into trouble. He had great leadership gifts and became known as 'father of the York clergy'. During his time, the church grew greatly, so much so that they had to put in a balcony to accommodate the numbers. One of the main reasons for this was that he, and others, had fine teaching gifts and as a result St Michael le Belfrey became known as something of a teaching centre in the north of England.

Churches that overflow – that is, churches whose influence extends beyond themselves as the Spirit of God flows out from them – often become teaching centres.

We saw in the previous chapter that the overflowing church of Antioch was a church of prophets. However, Luke is clear (in Acts 13:1) that alongside the prophets there were also 'teachers'. As the Lord raised up and gathered gifted teachers in this church, so it became a teaching centre for the region. This was one of its most important characteristics as it helped people mature as disciples. This was crucial to the church's growth and impact.

The influence of teaching

When the Spirit of Jesus comes and lives in our hearts, one of the things he does is put inside us a hunger for God's Word. His Word nourishes us and, as we cooperate with the Spirit, so we grow into the likeness of Christ. There is a longing to be taught. To be taught by gifted, godly, Spirit-filled people. That's why churches with such leaders often become teaching centres that grow. So, when Barnabas brings Saul to join him in the wonderful work taking place in Antioch during phase four of their growth, we're told:

> for a whole year [they] met with the church and taught great numbers of people. The disciples were called Christians first at Antioch (Acts 11:26).

Here we see a number of important things about teaching, things that were important in Antioch and should be in any future overflowing church.

First, teaching *is a long-term work.* We see that in Antioch. While there are some things in God's kingdom that are instant, many take time. Teaching is normally like that. The work is often slow but significant. By receiving regular teaching over a long period of time, we grow. It's rather like taking regular exercise. We don't see the benefit immediately, but over time it's worth it. Conversely, if we don't exercise we don't notice the difference straight away, but eventually we find we're getting flabby and unfit. So it is if we don't receive regular teaching from God's Word. We become spiritually unfit. To grow as a follower of Jesus we must read the Bible every day, allowing its truth to sink deep into our lives, and we must also receive regular teaching from gifted Bible teachers.

At The Belfrey we have a long legacy of good Bible teaching. Roger Simpson, who led the church immediately before me, was one such great teacher. His warm-hearted nature, combined with his evangelistic gifts, were used by the Lord to grow the church and to strengthen it as a teaching centre. We seek to continue that today, with preaching and teaching playing an important role in all our worship services. We recognise that the style may change in order to communicate effectively to a new generation, but the content is always biblical. We teach the Bible. Teachers should not teach their own good ideas, but the truth of God's unchanging Word, found in Scripture. Faithful Bible teaching is important and should be honoured. It's a crucial, slow work of the Holy Spirit.

Second, this work *often gathers good numbers of people.* That was certainly the case in Antioch. However, it's important to say that numbers are not always a sign of faithful Bible teaching. Numbers might be high simply because the church knows how to draw a crowd. Sometimes there are great teachers, working in villages where the population is not large, or whose teaching skills are not especially known, who are nevertheless faithfully and effectively teaching a small number of people week by week. Such faithfulness is one of the most important qualities for a teacher. Faithful teachers produce faithful people. The Lord loves to honour such faithfulness, and often he does so by attracting growing numbers of hungry people to be fed by excellent teaching.

Third, teaching *is central to discipleship.* Discipleship is the daily practice of following Jesus.[1] It's not coincidental that Luke describes *disciples* being called 'Christians' in the same sentence that he writes about *teaching*. That's because in Antioch they knew that discipleship and teaching go together, because one of the main ways we grow as disciples is through receiving and then applying good Bible teaching.

At The Belfrey we've run an internship programme for a number of years. We now do this as part of the New Wine Discipleship Year programme, which is a national scheme where young disciples are placed in churches for a year to grow in their discipleship. We lead one of the training hubs which gathers interns from various churches in our region on a Monday. When they meet together, the interns love to worship and pray. They spend time growing in friendship and fellowship. In fact, they'll do a variety of things to help them grow as disciples. But the main thing that happens is *teaching*. We are the regional teaching centre for this. We cover all sorts of subjects, aiming to help these young followers of Jesus grow in their love for Christ and their knowledge of his Word, seeking to equip them to be lifetime followers of Jesus. It's one way we are seeking to be an overflowing church, impacting our region.

Fourth, all teaching *should be Christ-centred.* Disciples of Jesus – of 'the Way', as it was originally called (Acts 19:9) – were first called 'Christians' in Antioch. That was a name given to them by those who were not Christians. It meant they followed the way of Jesus. They became apprentices to him – to the person and teachings of Christ. And the word 'Christian' still means this! While it's interesting to hear the thoughts, ideas and teachings of all sorts of people, Christians follow and seek to be taught by one person above all others – *Jesus Christ*!

That means we teach Christ. So, teaching centres should be all about Jesus. His life, death, resurrection and ascension have changed everything, including our own lives. Our forefathers knew this, redating history by his birth. We, too, in seeking to teach disciples must make sure that our teaching is centred on the God who has revealed himself to us in Jesus Christ.

One way we do this at The Belfrey is to stay prayerful. As teachers are preparing their messages, we ask them to do so prayerfully. Before someone speaks, we pray, calling upon Christ and asking him, by his Spirit, to communicate through the speaker so that Christ becomes our Teacher – our rabbi. After all 'rabbi' was one of the names he was most called during his earthly ministry.[2] At the end of any teaching we normally pray again, going into what's sometimes called 'ministry time', encouraging people to respond to God's Word and giving them an opportunity to receive prayer and be strengthened by God's Spirit. Prayer and teaching go together.

Gathering for teaching

As Antioch developed into a teaching centre for the region, so 'great numbers of people' (Acts 11:26) were taught and influenced. Such is the power and impact of God's Word. We're not told how this worked logistically. Perhaps at times they were taught in one large group, or perhaps in various congregations by Barnabas and Saul, as the numbers swelled. It's likely that they broke down into smaller groups, too, being taught in homes. We know from Acts 15:35 that they were not just taught by these two senior leaders but that 'many others taught and preached the word of the Lord' as well. This reminds us that teaching should be shared – which means teachers need to train other teachers to encourage further overflow – and that this can take place in all sorts of ways.

> Teaching should be shared – which means teachers need to train other teachers.

At The Belfrey we teach through Sunday congregations and through small midweek groups. We also put on various courses, have occasional teaching days and conferences. Like many churches our talks are recorded and put online for others to hear.[3] We've also experimented at live-streaming our services so that others can watch from overseas or catch up later. This is all part of our desire to be an overflowing church. That's why we also produce teaching books and why I also regularly write a discipleship blog[4] and leadership blog.[5] It's all part of overflow.

Teaching and preaching

As we've already seen, after the Jerusalem Council in AD50 which Barnabas and Paul attended, they returned to the overflowing church of Antioch with two of the leaders from the Jerusalem church – 'Judas (called Barsabbas) and Silas' (Acts 15:22) who 'were prophets' (v. 32). These two prophets stayed for a while, encouraging the church, before heading back to Jerusalem. What then happened to Paul and Barnabas? Luke is clear that they 'remained in Antioch, where they and many others taught and preached the word of the Lord' (Acts 15:35). They stayed there. They invested there. They poured their life and energy and faith and love into these people. They wanted the church to be strengthened, for the sake of overflow. How did they do it? They did it through teaching and preaching.

Some people make a distinction between teaching and preaching. Both are mentioned alongside each other in Acts 15, suggesting there is a distinction, although I wouldn't want to make too much of it. Most Bible commentators see *teaching* as explaining, while *preaching* is more heralding, declaring and exhorting.[6] Teaching often tends to aim more at the head, whilst preaching targets the heart. I know that I am more of a natural teacher than a preacher, but it's not always clear which I am doing when I stand up and talk, and that doesn't really bother me. I'm always seeking to improve at both, and creating tight categories is not always helpful as the best teachers also preach, and the best preachers also teach! I suspect this was the case at Antioch as, over time, the church became known as a teaching centre in the region.

Considerations for teachers

Sometimes people ask what kind of teaching might characterise a teaching centre, such as that at Antioch. We're not told how they taught in Antioch, but here are ten things we've been learning about teaching at The Belfrey. These are mentioned here not because we're experts at teaching. I certainly am not – and I know there are many who are more engaging Bible teachers than me. But our teaching is important to us, and over the years we've learned various lessons which are shared here in the hope they'll encourage churches who, like us, are seeking to grow and become effective teaching centres.

1. Teach from the Bible[7]

This means that the Bible should be opened, publicly read and then taught. That's why we have copies in church for all to read and refer to. We often teach through expository preaching, which means going through a Bible passage verse by verse. But sometimes it might be right to focus on just one verse, especially if the teacher has a prophetic sense to do that. Occasionally the teaching might be thematic, which would involve looking at a key passage and then a number of other passages too that fill out the theme. In all these ways, the Bible teacher should aim to say what the Bible says. And most importantly, as we teach the Bible – the written Word of God – we always point to Christ – who is the living Word of God. Even when teaching from the Old Testament, we would always want everyone to see that every Bible text finds its fulfilment in Christ. Without Jesus, the whole Bible does not make sense!

2. Prepare well[8]

When I prepare to teach in this way, I always read the passage a number of times first and as I do so, I make notes. I'm prayerfully asking the Lord to help me understand it and its meaning and to show me what to say and how to say it, so those listening can apply it to their lives. I look at the context. And I would often use commentaries too – but not straight away. I do this if there is something I am unsure about or to double check the meaning, but I normally recommend to budding teachers not to go too early to a commentary, as if you're not careful you'll just teach what the commentators say. A lot of my notes and things I look at in my preparation never actually get into my talk. They're the background to ensure that when I speak I'm confident in what I'm saying.

3. Be memorable[9]

It helps if people can remember key parts of the message, so it's worth using phrases or soundbites to summarise. Perhaps they're repeated for emphasis. They may be used as key points. You don't have to use soundbites, but it can help in your communication (especially in today's social media culture). But don't use soundbites just to be fashionable. Do it to be memorable. Using quotations from others can help in this too, including quotes from a wide variety of sources, especially people who are different to you (e.g. in gender, race, age and/or background). To help me in this I've developed, over a number of years, a quotes file[10] that now has hundreds of quotations from all sorts of people on lots of subjects. It's a great resource for me to use when I teach.

4. Don't be boring[11]

Sometimes teaching can be boring. That's why I recommend that teachers show early on that the Bible passage relates to real life today. There used to be a model of Bible teaching that encouraged the teacher to spend the first four-fifths of a talk explaining what the Bible meant when it was first written, and then the final fifth in contemporary application. Whilst that might have worked a few years ago, unless you're a really engaging teacher, most people have switched off by the time you get to the application, so I encourage teachers to apply early. Your listeners want to know that God has a message for them and that his Word applies to their daily lives. So tell a story. Use an illustration. Share a thoughtful quotation. This captures people's attention and makes them want to listen! Then ensure you keep applying the teaching to daily life, as you go through. If people can't see that the Bible really is relevant to their lives, they won't listen, they won't grow and they probably won't stay.

5. Use humour[12]

Many communicators use humour in their talks. J.John, one of the best-known Christian communicators in our nation is a great example of someone who uses humour brilliantly and effectively. I sometimes use humour when I speak, but to be honest I'm not a naturally funny person. I don't especially remember punchlines and don't tell lots of funny stories in life. So I don't put *lots* of jokes in my talks as I know it's not really 'me'. But I know that humour used well can really communicate, so if I can, I'll tell a funny story, as humour is another way of capturing people's attention and, when used wisely and carefully can really help communicate the message.

> Humour is another way of capturing people's attention.

6. Choose words carefully[13]

Whilst you don't have to work from a full script, it's important to think about the words you're going to use. At The Belfrey we aim to preach simply without being simplistic. This means not using long words or theological terms unless they're explained. We aim to ensure that someone brand-new to church with no Christian background will understand what's being said. If we're speaking on a sensitive subject it's really important to use words carefully, so as to avoid unintentional trouble.

7. Use media[14]

In today's multimedia world it can help to have a simple and clear PowerPoint or keynote presentation. However, sometimes people make great slides in order to cover up a poorly prepared message. Don't do that! And don't prepare a talk that's dependent on the slides, as your talk will dive if the slides don't work (which, as we know, sometimes happens!). When I prepare slides, they're to complement the message. If for some reason they don't work, that's OK. Sharing a choice film clip can similarly be helpful, as long as it's used prayerfully and well.

8. Know your audience[15]

It's good to have some idea of the background of those who will be listening, as this should affect the time-length of your talk and the type of illustrations used. So, if you can, get to know the age, gender and social background of your audience. Also don't assume everyone is a follower of Jesus.

9. Preach for a response[16]

Some teachers neglect to think about the response. If you want a growing and overflowing church, we've been learning at The Belfrey to think and pray much more about the response. The preachers of the eighteenth-century evangelical awakening did just this, preaching for a response. This starts with us not just asking in prayer, 'Lord, what do you want to *say*?' but also asking 'Lord, what do you want to *do*?' The answer to that question can guide not only what is said, but also how the talk closes and the response time that follows.

10. Invite people to start following Jesus[17]

At The Belfrey we pray daily that in our city and beyond people will be amazed by Christ and begin following him. As the Bible is publicly taught, we're hoping that the response for anyone present or listening online who's not yet following Jesus, will be to open their hearts and give their lives to him. So, it's usual now, whenever the Bible is taught, for the speaker (or service leader) to encourage people to start following Jesus. This can be done in all sorts of ways. What's important is to make the invitation because the more we do that, the more we're finding people are saying 'yes' and starting the exciting, challenging and rewarding journey of becoming disciples of Christ.

A couple of years ago I was speaking at a Christian festival in the north of England. Towards the end of my talk, I encouraged everyone, as they went home, to tell people about Jesus. I especially urged preachers to call people to give their lives to Christ. To illustrate this, I asked if there was anyone present who was not yet a believer, and would like to start. Two people indicated they would and so I led them in a simple prayer to commit their lives to Christ, and sent them off in the care of their local churches. A number of church leaders came up to me afterwards saying that at this festival where most people were probably already believers, they did not expect there'd be many or any who would want to do this, and it encouraged them, in their Bible teaching, to regularly encourage people to start following Jesus.

Such is the power of Bible teaching and the importance of inviting people to give their lives to Christ and start following him.

The risk of teaching

Occasionally I visit a church that's known for its teaching and find it rather dull. It's possible to be biblically sound but terribly dry and this can sometimes become

> It's possible to be biblically sound but terribly dry.

a risk of teaching centres. That's why Bible teachers need to be encouraged to devote good time and prayer to preparation, praying for the message to be fresh and relevant. They need the backing of intercessors, praying that the Word would touch hearts. And they need good feedback, to constantly be improving.

In his excellent book *5Q,* Alan Hirsch sees great value in teachers and how 'they will seek to bring theological truth and shape the consciousness of God's people to be consistent with that truth'. However, he also recognises that they 'often do not have that sense of urgency that drives the apostolic and prophetic functions'.[18] That means if teachers overdominate a church, they can slow it down, not wanting the church to move until everything has been taught and fully absorbed.

Another risk, of even greater concern, is the risk of legalism. Legalism is being so concerned about detail that the big picture is missed. It ends up producing what is sometimes called a 'works righteousness' rather than 'a righteousness that comes by faith'.[19] Teachers who become legalistic are so consumed by the truth of God's Word, urging people to conform to it, that they forget that the Lord is full of overflowing grace and forgiveness to those who fail. Such legalism often ends up making people feel guilty that they're not good enough or following the teaching of the Bible well enough. They 'speak the truth' but not 'in love'.[20] Legalistic teaching can be hard to break without a fresh outpouring of the Holy Spirit drenching parched hearts. That's why it's good to keep teaching and prophecy together. Teaching the truth of God's enduring Word in the power of the present Spirit is a fresh and potent cocktail mix that our loving Father loves to serve up!

Teaching and prophecy

Sometimes at The Belfrey people give their lives to Christ after hearing the Word of God read and expounded and also in response to a prophetic word. In our services we often share words, pictures and impressions about all sorts of people and situations that come as we pray before, or sometimes during, the service. Sometimes people ask for prayer in response to a word for healing for a specific condition or part of the body, and they encounter God's healing touch. If they're not yet a believer, they're now very open to finding out more or even ready to start following him. This combination of Bible teaching *and* prophetic ministry can be very transformative. It's a helpful reminder that when the two work in tandem, then it's a powerful combination which the Spirit of Jesus loves to use for overflow.

This shows us that teaching centres function best when the prophetic culture is strong. They're meant to go together and work together. That's what was happening in the overflowing church of Antioch. Indeed, it was these two ministries that the church was especially known for. When prophecy and teaching work together like this it may not always be clear whether what is happening is 'teaching' – sharing the enduring, ongoing Word of God – or 'prophecy' – communicating the immediate word of God for the here and now. That uncertainty is fine. Because in the end it's all the work of the one and the same Spirit.

When I was teaching recently someone came up to me and said that they'd appreciated my teaching and then they said, 'I think what you said may be a prophetic word for the church right now.' I said that I thought they were right. I hadn't said in the message that I felt the word was especially 'prophetic'. I obviously hadn't needed to!

The Spirit of Jesus has much to say to us and much to teach us. We need to listen to his voice. For Jesus Christ is the Great Teacher – the greatest teacher of all. He's also the best evangelist, and loves to empower the church to share the good news, as we'll see as we consider in the next chapter the gift of the evangelist.

Application: The gift of the teacher

Questions for disciples and church leaders to consider from this chapter:

1. To see if you might have teaching gifts, consider the following:
   - Do I particularly identify with Bible verses like these:

     'Preach the word; be prepared in season and out of season' (2 Tim. 4:2)

     'All Scripture is God-breathed, and useful for teaching, rebuking, correcting and training in righteousness' (2 Tim. 3:16)

     'not many of you should be teachers . . . because you know that we who teach will be judged more strictly' (Jas. 3:1)?

     Read the three scriptures quoted above and consider what they mean.
   - Think of someone known to you who is a fairly new believer, who might value some supportive teaching input from you. Pray for them right now, that they would grow in their knowledge and understanding of the faith. Then contact them and ask them if they'd like to meet with you to read the Bible together – perhaps over four sessions initially. If they say yes, then meet and suggest a simple plan of what you might do. Always pray with them, and also encourage them to spend some time every day reading the Bible and praying, and then seeking to live out the message in their lives.

2. If you think 'teacher' may be your dominant ministry:
   - Pray about this.
   - Find another teacher and talk with them about this.
   - Talk to your church leader about this.

3. If you are a church leader and see latent teaching gifts in someone:
   - Ask permission to lay hands on them and pray. If they agree, pray and ask the Holy Spirit to come and release all the gifts he has for them – particularly teaching gifts. Ask the Lord to provide, to equip and to enable.
   - Then invite the potential teacher to pray, asking the Lord to show them one person they could be helping to grow in their knowledge and understanding of the faith at present. (Note: it should normally be a person of the same gender.) Tell them to contact that person to see if they'd like to meet over a number of weeks to read the Bible together (as above).
   - Agree to meet with the potential teacher again in a month, for feed-back, so you can encourage them in their gifts.

Evangelistic Confidence:
The gift of the evangelist

In 2013, when there was a staff vacancy at The Belfrey for a senior leader to work alongside me, we wrote a job description describing the kind of work that person would do, and a person specification with the kind of personal qualities we were looking for in that leader.

I went to talk with the Bishop of Selby about the role and he said to me, 'Do you have anyone in mind for the role?' I said there was one person who, if he was available and would come, would be ideal, but other than that, I had no one specifically in mind from within the church or outside.

'Go and chat to them,' said the bishop, 'and see if they'll come. If they will, let's interview them first and see if the fit is good. If not, then advertise.'

So I went to see my friend and prayer-partner Greg Downes who, in my opinion, is one of the best evangelists[1] in our denomination and in the UK and, to cut a long story short, he was interested, was interviewed by a panel from church, then separately by the bishop, and was appointed. Greg brought great gifts of evangelism – gifts that I didn't have and gifts that we needed in our church. The appointment was timely and helpful.

After Greg was appointed, I remember reading Acts 11 and identifying so much with Barnabas. He needed help from a gifted evangelist and so went to Tarsus to find Saul, and brought him to the church in Antioch, to help with the work. I felt like the Lord had led me to do a similar thing in finding Greg!

Greg has now moved on from us, being very much called and sent out to work in Oxford at Wycliffe Hall, training missional clergy. Although Greg was only with us a few years, he left a good legacy, and in particular he helped raise our evangelistic confidence.

Oxford in the good news

Evangelistic confidence is something lacking in much of the Western church, including the UK church and much of the Church of England. Tolerance is a good quality in British culture, but it's been elevated in many circles as the highest virtue of all, with the result that some feel they cannot talk about certain issues – including Christian faith – for fear of offending others. Such a view, of course, can't be right, as living in a tolerant society should encourage freedom of speech, not constrain it! But many followers of Jesus do feel inhibited. They worry they might offend, or say the wrong thing, so they say nothing. While they long in their hearts for their friends and family to come to know Christ as they do, they fear being labelled a religious extremist. Some also don't know how to share their faith. Others, who've not seen anyone begin following Jesus for a long time, may doubt whether the good news of Jesus still works and is transformative. All this results in a lack of confidence in evangelism.

The gift which the evangelist brings challenges these wrong assumptions and helps individuals and churches grow in their evangelistic courage. This happens as they see the evangelist at work, and as they hear stories of changed lives. Then as more and more new baby believers are visible and vocal in church, so confidence grows in the gospel – in the good news of Jesus. Women and men who were once fearful start to see that they shouldn't be 'ashamed of the gospel, because' it really 'is the power of God that brings salvation'.[2] There's nothing like seeing the joy that new believers have from encountering Christ! It renews the faith of those who've been following Christ for a while, reminding us that Jesus really was right when he said: 'I am the way and the truth and the life. No one comes to the Father except through me.'[3]

My wife and I host a midweek small group in our home. There are a spread of ages and experience in the group, and when it gets too big, we multiply and form another. Over the last few years, quite a lot of those who've join our group have been brand-new believers. I like that. They come with all sorts of baggage and lots of questions. They're great for the group, being a constant reminder to us that Christ changes lives and really is the answer to every longing heart.

At the church in Antioch, I'm sure Saul was not the only one who did all the evangelism. He clearly had a great story to tell of his own conversion, and we know from the rest of the New Testament that he was gifted in sharing and explaining the good news, but also that he loved encouraging others to do the same. That means he would have looked for those with evangelistic gifts, and trained them. In doing these things I suspect he helped the church get even stronger in their evangelism. This is an important and often overlooked role of the evangelist.

Evangelists, of course, are to work outside the church. At The Belfrey we encourage our evangelists to be on the streets, to spend time in coffee shops and any place where people gather and to look for the opportunities God will give them to share their faith. This is really important. But evangelists also have a crucial role in encouraging the church in its evangelism.

Evangelism, according to Alan Hirsch is 'essentially the task of getting the message out and getting a positive response from the audience. In many ways, the evangelistic function is the church's inbuilt marketing department'.[4] Evangelists play a crucial role in this – in promoting the good news of Jesus and encouraging the rest of the church to do the same. That's why it says in Ephesians 4:11,12 that God appoints leaders, including evangelists, 'to equip' the rest of the church 'for works of service'. That means that evangelists need to help those who aren't evangelists become more evangelistic. This doesn't mean we all become evangelists, it just means we all grow in our confidence in sharing the good news. We want to seize all the opportunities God gives us in talking about Jesus.[5] Each time we talk about our faith we want to bring people nearer to Christ. We might even be the one who

> Evangelists need to help those who aren't evangelists become more evangelistic.

helps them take that first step of faith in welcoming Jesus into their life, or maybe someone else might do that. The main thing is that together we can all play our part in creating an evangelistic culture, where our faith spills out naturally. This is part of what it means to be a church of overflow. God's Spirit of mission equips and fills us so that evangelism flows out.

Evangelism in Antioch

There are all sorts of ways local churches can do this. We're not told in Acts how they did this in the church of Antioch – although I'd like to know! Maybe we're not told so we don't copy their techniques. It would be easy to do this, thinking there's a prescribed way, but when it comes to evangelism it's not so much about a technique but about genuinely loving people and showing our faith through our words and actions. The way we do this will change, depending on the context and on people's age, gender, background, culture and much more. In the end, what's most important is that the good news is shared.

If the good news is not shared, then there will be little or no evangelistic fruit. People will not find faith in Christ and the church will decline. Such is the history of churches that lose their first love for Christ and their heart for evangelism. Romans 10:14,15 says: 'How can they believe in the one of whom they have not heard? And how can they hear without someone preaching to them? And how can anyone preach unless they are sent?' Here we're reminded that God wants to raise up and send out gifted people who can preach and proclaim the good news of Jesus, to enable people to find faith. These people are called evangelists, and we need many more of them in our day.

Evangelism in the UK

As I look around the church in the UK today, I see many churches with few or no evangelists. Either they're there but their latent gifts are dormant or have been crushed, or they're not there because the leadership of the church has not prayed for, affirmed or encouraged the role of the evangelist. That's why I often urge local church leaders to pray that the Lord will raise up evangelists in their village, town or city. The church needs them. The lost need them.

I believe that in the coming days we will see more evangelists take their place in local churches. Some places will become especially known for this, as other evangelists are attracted there. These places will become centres of excellence where evangelists go for training and are then sent out. The church in Antioch became such a place, sending out Paul and Barnabas and others, as we know. We have been seeking to do this at The Belfrey. When Roger Simpson and I swapped jobs in 2010 and I became vicar, part of Roger's time was then spent doing evangelistic missions in our region as part-time Archbishop of York's Evangelist for the Northern Province. As more evangelists emerged at The Belfrey, particularly under Greg Downes's influence, so people like Paul Myers and Warren Furman have been raised up from us, and go out sharing the gospel, and give significant time to encouraging other churches in the north in their evangelism. Miriam Swaffield is an excellent young evangelist who's emerged from our daughter church G2 and has been recently living in Middlesbrough, sharing the good news in one of the most unchurched parts of our nation. It's been great to play a small part in seeing people come to faith in our region. I hope there is much more that we can do in the future, as we aim to see this ministry develop as the church in the north of England grows in its evangelistic confidence. It's all part of overflow.

Evangelistic personalities

As we look out for and seek to raise up more evangelists, it's good for us to know what kind of person we're looking for. Here's what we've found: there's not one type of evangelist.

> There's not one type of evangelist.

Sometimes we think evangelists will be extroverts. Not always. Often they are. But sometimes they're not. J.John is one of the most gifted and effective evangelists in our nation at present. On stage he presents as very outgoing, but when you get to know him he is a fairly quiet, reflective person who enjoys time on his own. That was true too of David Watson, the famous evangelist and previous vicar of The Belfrey in the 1970s.

Sometimes we think evangelists will be young. Maybe that's because young evangelists often draw a crowd. They can be good at catching people's attention, which can be very effective. But some of the best evangelists are old people. My elderly mother is in one of the most fruitful evangelistic periods of her life. And she is over 80!

Sometimes we think evangelists will be eloquent. That can help. Especially if you're the kind of evangelist who speaks in front of lots of people. But some of the best evangelists are those who work one-to-one. They simply chat with their friends and family about Jesus, and they're very good at it. They're not especially eloquent, but they have a story to tell and a passion to see others discover God's love in Jesus Christ. This passion is more important than eloquence.

Sometimes we think evangelists will be male. But the Bible presents many examples of female evangelists, such as the woman Jesus met at a well in Samaria, where 'Many of the Samaritans from that town believed in him because of the woman's testimony'.[6] When Jesus was born, the first evangelist after the male shepherds was an elderly woman called Anna, who 'spoke about the child to all'.[7] After the resurrection of Jesus, the first evangelists were women – 'Mary Magdalene, Joanna, Mary the mother of James, and the others with them who told [about it] to the apostles.'[8] Throughout church history it's often been women who are gifted as evangelists.

So, evangelists come in all sorts of shapes and sizes. They include a breadth of personality types. They can be of any age. They don't have to be great public speakers or well-educated. They can be of either gender, and come from a range of backgrounds. In the end, there's only one common thing about evangelists: they can't stop telling people about Jesus.[9] They are gifted in helping people see how amazing Jesus is

> There's only one common thing about evangelists: they can't stop telling people about Jesus.

and at encouraging them to make a decision for Christ. Outside the church, evangelists might often find themselves in a career in sales. They are good at gathering people with their compelling message. They're great at selling and sealing the deal. It's their gift.

The risk of evangelists

The risk of having evangelists in the church is that they will abuse their 'sales' gifts. Alan Hirsch hints at this, pointing out that evangelists 'tend to have an indefinable trait that goes beyond what they say and makes others want to agree with them'.[10] This gift is therefore open to misuse, especially as a means of making money. Evangelists are vulnerable to this, with the history of the church being littered with examples of evangelists being tempted by money. Wise evangelists and those mentoring them need to be aware of this, and test their motives. People in church who see women and men with evangelistic gifts often like to support them, as they want to get behind those who are helping bring others into God's kingdom. While this is understandable, evangelists need to take great care and for those who do this full-time, need to be accountable and transparent about their finances. It's one of many reasons why evangelists are best rooted in, and paid through, a local church as one of the five-fold ministries, rather than setting up their own para-church 'ministry' outside of a local church.

The other main risk of a church encouraging evangelists and becoming more and more evangelistic is that it will become so focused on winning new people for Christ that it forgets to care for and nurture those who are already followers of Jesus. This is why evangelism needs to be seen not as a ministry on its own but as part of the ministry of the local church and why evangelists, pastors and teachers need to work together in order to make and nurture disciples.

The benefits of evangelists

If we stop raising up evangelists and cease evangelising, the church will die. But more positively, evangelists help people begin the exciting journey of following Jesus. As such, evangelists bring much life to the local church. They bring faith. Energy. Vibrancy. Stories. They're like the trumpet-blower – the heralds – at the front of a liberating army, setting people free from an oppressive regime. They bring good news. To all. Their voices need to be heard, more and more in our day.

Acts 1:8 says that when God pours out his Spirit, there is an overflow in evangelism, with people going out to witness to Christ locally, regionally and internationally.[11] As we pray for a fresh outpouring of the Spirit today, we should be expecting more evangelism to happen and more evangelists to emerge. The fact that there seems to be a lack of evangelists in the UK church, and not many overflowing churches in the UK, is telling. That's why we need to be praying for the Lord to release again his life-giving Spirit and the gift of evangelism upon his church in our day. The answer to that prayer will change the church. It will make us more evangelistic. More outward-looking. More missional. It will enable us to become even more a church of overflow.

In this chapter we have seen that evangelism is crucial for the future of the church. But it's not enough. If God's Spirit is to overflow into our communities and we're to see whole regions transformed, we need evangelism to result in new church communities being formed. That's why in our next chapter we will focus especially on church planting and the need in our day for more resource churches.

Application: The gift of the evangelist

Questions for disciples and church leaders to consider from this chapter:

1. To see if you might have evangelistic gifts, consider the following:
   - Do I particularly identify with Bible verses like these:
     'As for us, we cannot help speaking about what we have seen and heard' (Acts 4:20)
     'Always be prepared to give an answer to everyone who asks you to give the reason for the hope that you have' (1 Pet. 3:15)
     'Stand firm then . . . with your feet fitted with the readiness that comes from the gospel of peace' (Eph. 6:15)?
     Read the three scriptures quoted above and consider what they mean.
   - Ask the Lord for evangelistic opportunities to open up, even today. Pray you would see them, seize them and make the most of them, speaking the truth in love.

2. If you think 'evangelist' may be your dominant ministry:
   - Pray about this.
   - Find another evangelist and talk with them about this.
   - Talk to your church leader about this.

3. If you are a church leader and see latent evangelistic gifts in someone:
   - Ask permission to lay hands on them and pray. If they agree, pray and ask the Holy Spirit to come and release all the gifts he has for them – particularly evangelistic gifts. Ask the Lord to provide, to equip and to enable.
   - Then invite the potential teacher to pray, asking the Lord for evangelistic opportunities to open up, even today. Pray they would see them, seize them and make the most of them, speaking the truth in love.
   - Agree to meet with the potential evangelist again in a month, for feedback, so you can encourage them in their gifts.

Resource Church:
The gift of the apostle

I had lots of questions. I was keen to discover and discern. There were so many things I wanted to ask people, and ask God. That's why my first eighteen months in York, from January 2009, was spent mainly observing and enquiring. I'd arrived as associate minister of St Michael le Belfrey knowing quite a lot about the church and its history, having previously written my Master's degree dissertation on the previous vicar, David Watson,[1] but I really wanted to get to know what the Lord was doing in the church *now* and discern what the Lord was calling the church to in the *future*. So Roger Simpson, the vicar, and I spent much time praying together and seeking the Lord. Roger had helped the church strengthen its evangelistic and missional roots, sum-marised around the strapline 'bring in, build up and send out' but I wanted to know 'why?'. Why were we doing this? What was the big vision behind everything? Why did we exist?

As we prayed, discerned and listened, we knew it had something to do with our region. We were based in York and called, like every local church, to reach out to our locality, but we also felt a growing responsibility for our region – the north of England. We could see much need in the north, which has one of the lowest churchgoing populations in Europe, and we sensed the Lord calling us to be one of the churches in our region who would step up and play our part in seeing renewal and revival in our region. Over time, and as we worked with the wider leadership, this became summarised in our vision: *serving God's transformation of the north.* We believe this is God's desire – for his kingdom to come and will be done in the north of England, as it is in heaven.

Some misunderstand such a vision. They think it's arrogant. I've had it suggested to me that it's about empire-building. But nothing could be further from the truth. It's about 'serving' what God is doing. It's about *his* work, *his* kingdom, *his* transformation. Or they think it suggests *we* are going to transform the north on our own – which, of course, is not what we mean. All God's work is about partnership and teamwork. We simply want to play our part in helping our region, because we believe the Lord is at work in the north. I've even had it suggested that it's un-biblical, because the New Testament knows only local churches serving their locality. 'How,' I've been asked, 'can a local church serve God's plan for a region?' Well, as we've been seeing in this book, the church in Antioch did just that! The good things that were happening in Antioch impacted the surrounding area. It was a local church which helped transform the region. The name often given today for a church that impacts its region, like the overflowing church in Antioch, is a *resource church*.

What! Us a resource church?

A *resource church* is a church of overflow. It's a church that positively influences and resources others, not just in its locality but in its region. The church in Antioch was a church like that. It couldn't contain what the Spirit of God was pouring in. It had to release it. This happened in lots of ways, but the most obvious was in sending out of church planters again and again to spread the good news of Jesus, as we saw in the last chapter. As a result, the church in Antioch became the resource base for much of the great missional work in that region and beyond.

During my time at The Belfrey, and especially since taking over as vicar, I've been seeking intentionally to shape us into a church rather like Antioch – into more of a resource church.[2]

My friend Ric Thorpe is the Bishop of Islington and is responsible for church planting in the Diocese of London with a brief also to assist churches and dioceses in England in their church planting. Ric is a great encourager and is a clear thinker with a strategic mind. One thing Ric has been doing in recent years has been encouraging the development of more resource churches in the Church of England, believing them to be one of the key components necessary for seeing not just towns and cities, but regions and nations transformed. A resource church does this by embracing its identity as a church which exists to resource others.

Characteristics of resource churches

UK resource churches share a number of characteristics. Here are seven:

1. Resource churches generously make their resources available to others

As noted in Chapter 3, overflowing churches give away. In my opinion this is probably the most basic and foundational characteristic of a resource church.[3] If generosity is not deeply embedded within the culture of the church, it will never become a resource church. Like the church in Antioch, such churches hold lightly to what God has given, wanting to steward well all that's been placed in their hands. We seek to do this in lots of ways at The Belfrey. Here are a few examples. Since 2009 all our senior staff have had written into their job descriptions that they're to give 10 per cent of their time to other churches and external ministry outside our church. Some have given much more than this. This tithing of time has benefited many others in our area. It's a simple but strategic way to resource others. Most of our staff and many of our church serve on teams at New Wine summer conferences. We love resourcing others in this way. As already noted, we run an internship programme at The Belfrey, which now includes people from other towns and cities in our region who come to us all day on a Monday to be trained at our discipleship hub before serving for the rest of the week back in their local churches. We see this as part of giving away and resourcing others.

2. Resource churches resource with prayer and purpose

The Antioch church knew that nothing of lasting significance happens without prayer, and we've been discovering that afresh at The Belfrey. As we've developed our House of Prayer and are learning again what it is to fast and pray for God's kingdom to come in our region, so we want prayer for transformation and revival to undergird all we do. It's why intercessors from our House of Prayer could be found praying in the auditorium during most of the Church of England's summer General Synod, recently held in our city. It's an honour to be invited to help in this way. As we sense again a fresh call to prayer, so we speak a lot about the importance of prayer. It's why I've written a book on prayer – to help equip God's people to pray. We still have much to learn about prayer at The Belfrey, which is why we're asking the Lord, like the disciples of old, to 'teach us to pray'.[4]

3. Resource churches embody a number of key reforming characteristics

These characteristics are rooted in Scripture and are seen in churches, such as the Antioch church, that through church history have influenced beyond themselves. Four key characteristics noted by Ric Thorpe are: *generosity*; *unity*; *audacity* and *humility*.[5] The first and third are more obviously pioneering qualities, whereas the other two are godly virtues that ensure what is done is deeply rooted in Christ and in the mission of the wider church. These values sustain the resource church to keep going for the long haul and when embodied together are powerful and highly missional.

Generosity is, of course, about giving away what's been given. This includes leaders, teams of people and all kinds of resources. This is at the heart of church planting. *Unity* is about partnership, ensuring that resource churches work closely with bishops and church authorities and other churches in the area, because God wants to use all to extend the kingdom and there is no place for mavericks. *Audacity* is about bravely acting on the vision and strategy God gives. It produces the faith and courage to step out and have a go! Without such pioneering characteristics, churches will fear giving away and they'll not overflow. *Humility* is about sacrificially serving the city and being obedient to the Holy Spirit. This is exemplified in prayer and a desire by resource church leaders not for personal gain or status but for God's Kingdom to expand and impact the surroundings.

At The Belfrey we also have four key values. We agree with and share all of Ric's four qualities, especially identifying with and naming *generosity* and *humility* as central to who we are. So, for us, *generosity* is about increasingly becoming a church that gives away (as described in Chapter 3), and *humility* is about staying prayerful (see Chapter 2) and humble, working with others and recognising that all the work is the Lord's. To these two we have also added *festivity* and *simplicity*. *Festivity* is about developing a joyful church – the kind of church seen in Antioch (and outlined in Chapter 4). *Simplicity* is about not overcomplicating things. It's about doing the basics well, staying focused and clear and not trying to do everything or please everybody. These four values – of *generosity*, *humility*, *festivity* and *simplicity* – are shaping our church culture.

At times we've sought to do too much at The Belfrey and that's not been helpful. That's why it's good to have a clear strategy. (We will look in the next chapter at four strategic emphases we've developed, which are helping us embrace simplicity and to increasingly stay focused.)

4. Resource churches grow large, young and contemporary

Resource churches which embrace these reforming characteristics are, like the church in Antioch, normally growing churches which become large.[6] Indeed, resource churches need to grow, so they can regularly give away. While all ages are welcome, most resource churches in the UK today intentionally aim young, especially targeting the 18 to 30s. The young are open to change, are full of ideas, are often enthusiastic and willing to try new things and are a great source of fresh leadership. That's why UK resource churches are often found in cities where there's a good concentration of young people and probably at least one university. In order to attract the young and to communicate effectively, resource churches are normally contemporary in style and use colloquial language, using the best of modern music, film, graphic design and creative media. For us at The Belfrey, this has meant significant investment in staff with media expertise and an ongoing commitment to step up our contemporary communication each year. This is an ongoing challenge!

Given that the 18 to 30s are the least represented demographic in most UK churches, encouraging resource churches which reach this age group is surely a good thing! This age group is very open to new and innovative ways of doing things, which keeps resource churches fresh and interesting.

5. Resource churches are centres of vocational and leadership development

A resource church full of young people, brimming with energy, faith and ideas is a great breeding ground for young leaders. The benefit of the young is that they have energy and enthusiasm, vigour and vision, and are often flexible and fun-loving, probably having less commitments than older people. As these young leaders are identified, encouraged and given leadership experience – through good mentoring, leading small groups, with some joining an internship scheme – so a leadership pipeline begins to be created for the future. This is not just for church leadership, but is about equipping young leaders to lead well in every sector of society, including business, education, the arts, media and entertainment. Maybe some kind of leadership pipeline was also developed in Antioch, thus equipping the 'many others' referred to in Acts 15:35, who 'taught and preached the word of the Lord' alongside Barnabas and Saul.

6. Resource churches revitalise and plant

As resource churches grow, so there comes a point when the Lord sends people out to impact the region with the good news of Jesus. Two thousand years ago, this happened to the church in Antioch with Barnabas and Saul being sent to preach the gospel and start new churches in all sorts of towns and cities. Today, this might similarly involve starting a brand-new community. The Belfrey did this in 2004, starting G2, a fresh expression of church in York which is now one of the larger churches in our city. In today's so-called post-Christian world, it may also involve revitalising an old existing church, which normally means sending a leader and team to restart a church, bringing with them the mindset of overflow and the vision and desire to see the church grow again. Resource churches are passionate about revitalising existing churches and planting new ones.

7. Resource churches work strategically with church authorities

Finally, resource churches do not exist in isolation. They should work alongside other churches and ministries in their city and seek to be in good relation with these churches. Most importantly, they should exist and work under the authority of their own church leaders. In the Anglican Church of which I and The Belfrey are part, this is under the diocesan bishop. Bishops are the leaders in mission in their diocese. They have an apostolic call to 'proclaim afresh in each generation' the faith passed down to them. As resource churches are becoming more widely acknowledged and encouraged in the Church of England, so they're playing a part in refreshing this apostolic calling of the bishop and their diocese. So, resource churches must work with their bishops (or equivalent denominational leader), ensuring that what they do is supported by the bishop. This means honouring the bishop's leadership of the diocese and working strategically with the bishop and diocesan senior staff.[7] When this is done well, with the bishop and resource church working closely together, great things can be done.[8]

Perhaps we see something of this creative partnership going on between the local church and those in central authority in Acts 11:22ff, when Barnabas is sent to Antioch by the senior leaders in Jerusalem and then becomes the church leader. We don't know if Barnabas was imposed on the Antioch church, resulting in some negativity from the church, or whether they gladly accepted him. Or perhaps he came and negotiated with them and was invited by them to be their leader. It would be interesting to know how this happened, but we don't! What is clear, though, is that in the end they found a way through so that everyone was happy. This is a good reminder to any resource church of the importance of working closely, strategically and prayerfully with others, for the sake of the growth and mission of God's church.

Apostolic people

The mission of the church is advanced as people are sent out to pioneer. This is how the good news of Jesus has always spread. People sent out like this, according to the Bible, are called 'apostles', based on the Greek word *apostolos*, which literally means 'sent-out one'.[9] We should not mix up such people with the very first twelve apostles who, as Alan Hirsch clearly states 'played a unique, unrepeatable, irreplaceable role in the establishment of the original church.'[10] Nor should we give them the same authority as those who became Scripture-writers.[11] But there are nevertheless people described in the Bible as 'apostles' who were simply sent out as pioneers to start a new work.[12] That's why Ott and Wilson in their comprehensive textbook on church planting say 'the term *apostle* can be considered a rough equivalent to *missionary*'.[13] The New Testament names such people, and they include Andronicus,[14] Timothy and Silas,[15] Epaphroditus,[16] Andronicus and Junia.[17] In order to make the distinction, Alan Hirsch calls these people 'little "a" apostles', as opposed to 'the big "A" Apostles – the original twelve' and Scripture-writers.[18] These 'little "a" apostles' were people sent out to break new ground and establish churches. This, of course, is what Barnabas and Paul did – both in Antioch as they played a crucial role in establishing it and turning it into a church of overflow, and then elsewhere as they were sent out to preach the gospel and plant churches. That's why it shouldn't surprise or shock us to discover that in Acts 14:14 Luke also calls Barnabas and Paul 'apostles'.

It's noteworthy that God didn't just send one person. They went as a team – the two of them – also with John Mark.[19] It's possible the team might have included more, given that Luke also describes this missionary cohort as 'Paul and his companions'.[20] When Jesus had sent people out he'd always sent them out as a team, either as a group or in pairs.[21] This enabled them to share the prayer, the work and the responsibility. It kept them accountable and less likely to make silly decisions. It must also have been much more fun! In the same way that disciples are never called to follow Jesus on their own, so apostles are always meant to work in teams. Even if there's a designated leader, the leader must gather a team to work with. Effective evangelists and church planters today know how important it is to work with others. It's all about teamwork!

Apostolic calling

While teamwork is important, the call to be an apostle usually comes to an individual and can be very personal and sometimes dramatic. This was the experience of Paul, who knew at his conversion that he was called to be an apostle. Sometimes when someone has a powerful conversion experience, the Spirit of God communicates clearly to them about their future and divine calling. This happened to Paul around the year AD33/4. He was still called Saul then, and the story is recorded for us by Luke in Acts 9:

> Meanwhile, Saul was still breathing out murderous threats against the Lord's disciples. He went to the high priest and asked him for letters to the synagogues in Damascus, so that if he found any there who belonged to the Way, whether men or women, he might take them as prisoners to Jerusalem. As he neared Damascus on his journey, suddenly a light from heaven flashed around him. He fell to the ground and heard a voice say to him, 'Saul, Saul, why do you persecute me?'
>
> 'Who are you, Lord?' Saul asked.
>
> 'I am Jesus, whom you are persecuting,' he replied. 'Now get up and go into the city, and you will be told what you must do.'
>
> The men travelling with Saul stood there speechless; they heard the sound but did not see anyone. Saul got up from the ground, but when he opened his eyes he could see nothing. So they led him by the hand into Damascus. For three days he was blind, and did not eat or drink anything.
>
> In Damascus there was a disciple named Ananias. The Lord called to him in a vision, 'Ananias!'
>
> 'Yes, Lord,' he answered.

The Lord told him, 'Go to the house of Judas on Straight Street and ask for a man from Tarsus named Saul, for he is praying. In a vision he has seen a man named Ananias come and place his hands on him to restore his sight.'

'Lord,' Ananias answered, 'I have heard many reports about this man and all the harm he has done to your holy people in Jerusalem. And he has come here with authority from the chief priests to arrest all who call on your name.'

But the Lord said to Ananias, 'Go! This man is my chosen instrument to proclaim my name to the Gentiles and their kings and to the people of Israel. I will show him how much he must suffer for my name.'

Then Ananias went to the house and entered it. Placing his hands on Saul, he said, 'Brother Saul, the Lord – Jesus, who appeared to you on the road as you were coming here – has sent me so that you may see again and be filled with the Holy Spirit.' Immediately, something like scales fell from Saul's eyes, and he could see again. He got up and was baptised, and after taking some food, he regained his strength.

Paul's conversion and calling story is unique to him. And yet because it is written up in detail[22] and plays such a significant role in the book of Acts and the missional expansion of the early church, I think Luke presents it as a model apostolic calling.[23] That means there are things from this story that apply not just to Paul's apostolic calling but to others also called to be pioneers. Four things especially stand out.

First, apostolic pioneers are called to *surrender*. Saul had not been living for Christ. In fact, he'd been doing the very opposite and persecuting those who followed Jesus. Now he was called to be fully devoted to Christ. His encounter on the road to Damascus which resulted in him falling to the ground, temporarily losing his eyesight and having to be led into the city by hand was not just humbling. It was a sign of how God had plans to use Saul as someone surrendered to his apostolic purposes as a strategic servant of Jesus Christ.[24] Apostles and church planters today similarly know that God has called them to lay down their agenda, and follow Jesus.

Second, apostolic pioneers are called to *significance*. The Lord made it clear, through Ananias, that Saul was God's 'chosen instrument to proclaim [God's] name to the Gentiles and their kings and the people of Israel' (9:15). Most apostolic leaders know they're called to something important in God's kingdom, which involves pioneering and breaking new ground. They know they have a job to do and usually feel a profound sense of destiny.

Third, apostolic pioneers are called to *suffer*. No follower of Jesus is promised an easy life.[25] It's a great life[26] but also a life of challenges.[27] Apostles are especially called to take up their cross and to suffer as they pioneer for the gospel, with Saul being told by Christ at his conversion 'how much he must suffer for my name'.[28] Some of these sufferings were experienced by Paul in Antioch. Interestingly, no such sufferings in Antioch are mentioned in Luke's accounts in Acts. We only become aware of them from Paul's letters, as he later wrote to Timothy of the 'persecutions' and 'sufferings' that 'happened to me in Antioch'.[29]

And fourth, apostolic pioneers are especially empowered by the *Spirit*. After his initial encounter with Christ, which resulted in falling, becoming blind and hearing the audible voice of Christ, Saul then prayed fervently (9:11) in response to a vision (9:12); was prophesied over by Ananias (9:17); was healed of his blindness, filled with the Holy Spirit and baptised in water (9:18). Apostolic leaders often have dramatic encounters with the Spirit of Jesus, sometimes not unlike this, both at conversion and at other times too. These Spirit-encounters em-

> Apostolic leaders often have dramatic encounters with the Spirit of Jesus.

power and equip them for their apostolic leadership.

So apostolic leaders are called. While everyone's call is unique, most apostolic people would identify with these four big themes which we see in Paul's conversion and apostolic calling story. Ché Ahn, in chapter one of his fascinating book, *Modern-Day Apostles*, describes his own call to apostolic leadership. The chapter closes with these simple words: 'God calls apostles, and this is how he called me . . . If he has called you, that calling must be stewarded as something that is very important, something that is very valuable.'[30] In essence, pioneers like this need to live in the light of their call to apostolic leadership.

Apostolic leadership

A number of metaphors are used to describe an apostolic leader in the Bible. These include: planter, architect, foundation-layer, father and ambassador.[31] Interestingly, when I've listened to and talked to church planters today about what they're trying to do, they often use these kind of metaphors. Behind these various images is a strong missional desire in the leader to see women and men give their lives to Christ and for churches to be established. That's because true apostolic leaders get things started. They establish the church, which is why Paul in Ephesians 2:20 says that the church 'is built on the foundations of the apostles and prophets'. These words of Paul have traditionally and rightly been applied to 'big "A" apostles' and the establishment of the universal church. But I see no reason why they can't also be applied to 'little "a" apostles' and the establishment of local churches. This makes sense of what we've been seeing in this chapter about apostolic ministry and, as we saw in Chapter 5, about prophetic ministry. Both are foundational ministries which are very helpful when getting local churches started.

One Tuesday morning in 2017, while away speaking at a conference, I had a telephone conversation with Mark Tanner, the Bishop of Berwick, asking if The Belfrey could help plant a resource church in the northern city of Newcastle. This was an exciting but also challenging prospect. Was this something we should do? As he talked on the phone and as I began to pray about this at the end of the call, I felt convinced almost at once that this was not just a good idea by the bishop, but something the Lord was particularly calling us to do. How come? Because just a few minutes before Mark had contacted me, I'd received a text message from Richard Dearden, who heads up prophetic ministry at The Belfrey, sharing a prophetic picture he felt the Lord had given him that very morning in prayer – which was about people spilling out of us and going to a different city to plant a church! The timing was so helpful.

Not only that, but in case I needed reassuring that the Lord would provide people for us as some left to go on this new venture, I received two further texts that morning. One was describing how a number of people in York had decided to follow Jesus the previous Sunday in church, of which I was unaware. The other was of someone that very morning who had given their life to Jesus Christ! It was like the Lord was showing me that he could easily fill us up again with newcomers, and that I should not fear losing people to the plant. It felt like the *apostolic* call and *prophetic* word were coming together to guide us in the right direction. As a result, we're thrilled to have sent out Ben Doolan and a great team of people to lead this exciting plant in Newcastle, as we play our part in serving God's transformation of the north.

Acts 13:1–3 similarly shows how the *apostolic* call and *prophetic* word came together when the Lord called for new churches to start. The Antioch church was worshipping and as they did so a prophetic word came, that Barnabas and Saul should go and start new churches. No doubt this was confirmed and tested and resonated with not only Barnabas and Saul but also with the church. So, they went, as apostles – literally 'sent-out ones' – knowing they had a prophetic call from God. This would have given them confidence as they stepped into the unknown, knowing the Lord was not just with them in a general sense but *particularly* asking them to embark on *this* venture. All the people who became followers of Jesus, and all the churches they started were built on the foundation of the apostolic calling and prophetic word that came from Antioch. The result, according to Luke, was that 'the word of the Lord spread through the whole region'.[32] I suspect it was unsettling and very exciting – both at the same time!

Church growth and apostolic risk

We can say, then, that the church in Antioch was an apostolic community that created further apostolic communities. Another way to say this is that the church in Antioch was a church plant that also planted churches. This is very important and crucial to resource churches, because *resource churches plant churches that plant churches.* If this can be done again and again, then future growth becomes not just growth by addition, but growth by multiplication. If a resource church plants one church every year for ten years but none of those churches plant, then the simple maths shows that ten churches will have been planted by the end of Year Ten and by the end of Year Twenty the number will be twenty. If, however, the resource church can plant churches that within a few years can themselves plant churches, then by Year Ten perhaps fifteen or more new churches will have formed. If this continues, by the end of Year Twenty the number could be fifty-plus churches. The potential for growth is immense!

This kind of growth by multiplication is what happened in the churches planted from the overflowing church of Antioch. Church communities multiplied. There is no reason why the same cannot happen in the UK today. It's happening elsewhere: in India;[33] in Mozambique[34] and in many other places across the world. It's happening right now. As apostolic leader and church planter Heidi Baker says: 'There doesn't seem to be any limit to the number of churches we can plant if we have enough provision and people to help.'[35] If you visit areas where exponential church growth is happening, or read books about the work, it soon becomes clear that with growth comes mess. Church growth, especially growth by multiplication led by apostolic leaders, is not tidy. While such growth needs leading and guiding and good governance, it does not need to be overmanaged. Bringing too much bureaucratic control invariably stops growth, although this may not be seen for a while as growth brings with it a certain amount of momentum that rolls on for some time.[36]

One biblical picture of apostolic leadership which I love is that of the ox. We see Paul using it in 1 Timothy 5:18 in relation to leadership. An ox is a strong and sturdy animal which leads the way at the front of the plough, pulling the weight as the field is ploughed ready for growth. Proverbs 14:4 says:

Where there are no oxen, the manger is empty, but from the strength of the oxen come abundant harvests.

This reminds us that apostolic leaders, like oxen, are gifted to help churches grow and plant not just once, but again and again. They're meant to help produce abundant harvests. Their role is to have a regular overflowing impact on their region. Take the oxen away and the manger is empty. Everything is nice and tidy. The stable might look neat and orderly. But there's no growth. So it is with the pioneer leaders in church. If we want to see multiplication, then we need apostolic leadership which inevitably will create messy, untidy church.[37] That's how it's meant to be!

> If we want to see multiplication, then we need apostolic leadership.

At times, apostolic leaders can fall out with each other. Because they tend to be strong characters, often knowing how they want things to be and who they want on their team, they can sometimes be forceful in personality. This can result in team disagreement. That happened in Antioch and an example, as we've seen, is given us at the end of Acts 15. Barnabas and Paul, probably towards the end of AD49, were gathering a team so they could return to the churches they had visited in Acts 13 and 14. Barnabas wanted to take John Mark with them, whereas Paul didn't. Paul's apostolic nature came to the fore as he would not back down. He refused to take John Mark on the journey. Luke writes about this, saying that 'they had such a sharp disagreement that they parted company'[38] resulting in Barnabas taking Mark with him to Cyprus, while Paul took Silas to the churches they'd previously planted in Syria and Cilicia.[39] With the best will in the world, apostolic leadership can sometimes do this. It can sometimes unintentionally bring division and disagreement. We do not know if Paul and Barnabas ever fully reconciled, although we do know from 1 Corinthians 9:6 (written about AD54) that Paul speaks well of Barnabas, describing him as a fellow apostle, and that when writing to the Colossians (in 4:10, written round AD62) Paul refers to Barnabas in his letter without any sense of negativity. Also, towards the end of his life, Paul's letters show him asking for Mark to come to him.[40] It would be good to think that Paul and Barnabas eventually made up!

Another significant disagreement happened in Antioch just before this, probably in AD48. Paul was back in Antioch after his First Missionary Journey, when Peter arrived – perhaps as a travelling missionary[41] – and enjoyed fellowship with the Antioch church. After his vision in Joppa, Peter was pleased to interact with Gentiles as well as Jews, but it seems that while in Antioch he came under the influence of some from Jerusalem who were insisting that Gentile believers needed to be circumcised, and so Peter withdrew and only spent time with Jewish believers. Paul describes all this in Galatians 1, saying that 'even Barnabas was led astray'.[42] Paul was incensed, and wasn't afraid to use all the force of his intellectual and apostolic authority, to challenge Peter. We assume that Paul won the argument, but we don't actually know from Galatians 1 if that was the case. Certainly, the Jerusalem Council (of AD50) brought much needed clarity on this issue, but before then the position of the church was far from clear. It was around this time, probably just after the Paul/Peter controversy and before the Jerusalem Council, that similar trouble on this issue also erupted in Galatia, in one of the churches Paul and Barnabas had planted, resulting in Paul writing his robust Galatian letter to them. Paul needed all his apostolic gifts to navigate these difficult matters.

For all its strengths, apostolic leadership also has the potential to be abused and go off the rails, particularly through misuse of power. Because 'apostolic types tend to favour the entrepreneurial edge of the church and have a natural tendency for adventure'[43] they can push the church into new ventures that the church may not yet, or ever be, ready for. That's why they need to be prayerful people, and listen to the prophets. Apostolic leaders tend to have clear vision, walking with a real sense of purpose. This instils confidence in those around them. They often have a mix of gifts and their ministry is usually accompanied by signs and wonders. As a result, they are normally people-gatherers and people follow them. Sometimes people follow them as they move on to new places, pioneering new communities of faith, which is what they love to see. Churches led by apostolic leaders tend to grow. When this is going well, it's wonderful. But the risk of misusing apostolic gifts and influence is great. That's why, like other leaders, apostolic people need to live in a close relationship with Christ and to seek to live as his humble servants. If they stop praying and begin to think their ministry can thrive without reliance on the Holy Spirit of God, they are in for a mighty fall, and as they descend they will probably take others down

> Apostolic leaders tend to have clear vision, walking with a real sense of purpose.

with them. The devil loves to bring down apostolic leaders. They need our prayers.

I've been praying for some time for a fresh release of leaders in the UK church of our day, especially those with apostolic gifts. Without apostolic leadership we won't see new churches, especially vibrant resource churches, multiply and overflow, playing a key role in the transformation of regions.

We need to release apostolic leaders to plant churches that plant churches. That's at the heart of the vision of the resource church. For this to happen, resource churches need to pray and work strategically. We're learning about this at The Belfrey, and so in our final section I offer some reflections on our journey so far, identifying four strategic emphases that are proving helpful to us.

Application: The gift of the apostle

Questions for disciples and church leaders to consider from this chapter:

1. To see if you might have apostolic gifts, consider the following:
   - Do I particularly identify with Bible verses like these:
     'Then I heard the voice of the Lord saying, "Whom shall I send? And who will go for us?" and I said, "Here am I. Send me!"' (Isa. 6:8)
     'So after they had fasted and prayed, they placed their hands on them and sent them off' (Acts 13:3)
     'God has appointed in the church, first apostles . . .' (1 Cor. 12:28)?
     Read the three scriptures quoted above and consider what they mean.
   - Look back on your life. Do you love to pioneer things? In particular, have you started something that people get behind and follow?
   - If you're not leading something in your church (like a small group), ask your church leader if you can start doing this. You might need to receive some training. Start gathering people and see if it grows. Keep learning and stay accountable.

2. If you think 'apostle' may be your dominant ministry:
   - Pray about this.
   - Find another apostle and talk with them about this.
   - Talk to your church leader about this.

3. If you are a church leader and see latent apostolic gifts in someone:
   - Ask permission to lay hands on them and pray. If they agree, pray and ask the Holy Spirit to come and release all the gifts he has for them – particularly apostolic gifts. Ask the Lord to provide, to equip and to enable.
   - If they're not leading something in church (like a small group), ask them to start doing this. You or others might need to give some basic training. Encourage them to start gathering people, to see what grows, and to keep learning. Ensure they stay accountable.
   - Agree to meet with the potential apostle again in a month, for feedback, so you can encourage them in their gifts.

PART THREE

STRATEGIES FOR OVERFLOW

Evangelism, Discipleship, Leadership, Planting

Although the term 'resource church' may be new to some, the idea is old, as 2,000 years ago the church of overflow in Antioch became a resource church for their region. However, there's not just one kind of resource church described in the New Testament. There are a number. That means that not every resource church will look or work exactly like the church in Antioch, or for that matter like any other church (including The Belfrey in York). We need all sorts of churches to reach all sorts of people!

Resource churches in the New Testament

Back in the first century as the good news of Christ was spreading, the New Testament describes at least seven key resource-type churches which became strategic centres for the faith and whose influence overflowed to their surrounding area.

The first was the first-ever Christian community – the church in Jerusalem. This church grew to a large size. The outpouring of the Spirit on the Day of Pentecost kick-started it to an initial congregation of 3,000[1] and from there it grew to 5,000[2] and continued to increase in size.[3] We would today call it a mega-church. It was very Jewish in flavour and we read in Acts 2:42–47 and 4:32–35 that it was full of life and vitality. This church was obviously a resource church in the sense that all future churches flowed from this one! But there is little New Testament evidence to show that they were a great church-planting fellowship. They may have become this later, perhaps learning from the example of Antioch and beyond. Instead, the Jerusalem church was, at least initially, an attractional church, where people came to be healed, encouraged and built up in their faith before returning back home.[4] It became the centre from which the core apostles were based[5] and the place where key decisions of the church were made or ratified.[6]

The second was the church in Antioch, as we've been discovering.

After Antioch, we see further resource churches developing in a number of key cities. One was in Philippi. This third example of a resource church was the first church planted in Europe. It was built on the foundations of the apostolic leadership of Paul and Silas and prophetic revelation which came though the vision given to Paul of a man of Macedonia, begging him to 'come over . . . to help us'.[7] This church, like other resource churches was a church that gave away. They gave financially[8] and as they grew, they gave away people, with Ephesus becoming the launch pad for evangelism and church planting in Macedonia and into Europe.[9]

Another, and fourth, important resource church was found in Thessalonica, which also became a centre from which the gospel went out into the rest of Macedonia and Achaia. This multiethnic church, recognised for its generosity[10] also became widely known for its quality of fellowship and love,[11] and in the midst of opposition probably developed into something of a decentralised network of churches, rather like much of the underground Chinese church today, which tends to work well under persecution.

Corinth was a fifth important city where a key resource church developed. It was planted by Paul,[12] who began the work by investing time in a couple called Aquila and Priscilla. Aquila, like Paul, was a tentmaker. It's unclear whether this couple were already followers of Jesus, or whether they were the first converts in the city. Like he later did in Ephesus, Paul invested much time – more than one and a half years – in Corinth and establishing an overflowing resource church there.[13] The church was then nurtured by Apollos[14] and became very charismatic in personality and spirituality. Paul encouraged this church in its generosity. He knows that overflowing churches need to 'excel in this grace of giving' – modelled particularly through giving money.[15] It was through Corinth that further churches were launched in the region of Achaia.

A sixth New Testament resource church is seen in Ephesus. This became the apostolic base for ministry into Asia Minor. It is a little unclear from Acts 19 how this church began. It may have been planted directly by Paul during his Second Missionary Journey,[16] although it might have been initially started by Apollos, with the help of Paul's companions Priscilla and Aquila, who Paul brought with him from Corinth.[17] Certainly Paul invested a huge three years of his life there during his Third Missionary Journey, and so must have thought it to be strategic![18] Paul also decided that he would not raise up a local person to take responsibility for this church but rather leave there one of his key apprentices, Timothy, to be the resource church leader of this overflowing church.[19] It looks like the Ephesian church was a somewhat decentralised network of missional communities, committed to growth and expansion. From Ephesus many churches were planted. For example, Epaphras was sent from there to begin churches back in his home town of Colossae,[20] and probably also in Laodicea and Hieropolis.[21] It seems that Paul was establishing churches that could flourish without dependence on him, or the sending church. He no doubt realised that these were the kind of churches that had the greatest potential for multiplication.

Finally, Rome developed into a resourcing centre for Italy and beyond. Paul did not start this church, although he knew many of the believers[22] and would later serve and live there, ending his life in this city.[23] The church was probably founded by people Paul had led to Christ, along with some apostolic church planters who had moved there who were not disciples of Paul.[24] In the practical closing chapters of his epistle to them, Paul encourages them in their generous lifestyle[25] and in their gospel proclamation.[26] Neil Cole describes this church as 'an urban network of organic house churches in a major city'[27] and sees it as an interesting model for multiplication today.

It seems therefore that there was much flexibility of how resource churches grew and structured themselves. They probably developed unique personalities and shapes, while sharing the generous missional DNA poured out at Pentecost and exemplified so well in Antioch. They all sought to overflow with the good news of Christ to their city and region, wanting to give away the gospel and see men and women put their faith in Christ and new churches planted.

At The Belfrey, as we've sought to be faithful to the Holy Spirit's leading – and been especially inspired by the overflowing resource church in Antioch – so we've established four strategic emphases to help us fulfil the vision the Lord has given us for our region. These are to help us plan and work so that our vision of serving God's transformation of the north can be realised. Without these strategic emphases, our vision is just a fanciful dream. We believe God wants to turn vision into reality, which is why strategy is so important. Strategy gives us focus and helps us allocate our resources well. These four emphases are:

- EVANGELISM   making disciples
- DISCIPLESHIP   nurturing disciples
- LEADERSHIP   developing leaders
- PLANTING   planting churches

This chapter will focus on these four areas and on why these are important in today's missional context.

Evangelism

Jesus' last orders – his Great Commission – to his disciples were to 'go and make disciples of all nations, baptising them in the name of the Father and of the Son and of the Holy Spirit'.[28] The call to disciples to make more disciples is basic and intrinsic to our calling as followers of Jesus. This call, burning in the hearts of the disciples in Antioch, was what motivated them to tell neighbours, friends, work colleagues and anyone else, about the good news of Jesus. Today we call this evangelism.[29]

As we've seen in Chapter 7, evangelism is the responsibility of the church. Some are especially good and gifted at it, and we often call these people 'evangelists'. They just can't stop telling people about Jesus! Barnabas brought Saul to Antioch because he saw the need for a good evangelist to help with the work. We have a number of good evangelists at The Belfrey and in recent years we've seen an increase in numbers of people coming to faith as they go about their work. However, I sense there is much more evangelistic fruit the Lord has for us in York, and many more evangelists he wants to equip and release.

As I look out at the UK church, I do not see many evangelists. It seems the 'evangelist' is a much-neglected office in the church. The voice of the evangelist has been muffled. This must change. I also sense that in lots of British churches there's a lack of evangelistic boldness. I even see it in myself sometimes. The fear of looking foolish or offending others is powerful, so much so that many followers of Jesus say nothing about their faith, despite statistics showing that there are lots of people who are open and interested.[30] So it's time for the message of the evangelist to be heard again in every local church and in the shops and streets of our towns and cities. They also need to be released in our resource churches.

> It seems the 'evangelist' is a much-neglected office in the church.

When a church has a number of gifted evangelists sharing the good news and the church is regularly seeing people come to faith in Christ, it creates an atmosphere of expectation in the church. That's good and it creates a hunger for more. However, it's then easy for the rest of that church to become complacent, leaving the task of evangelism to those who seem especially gifted. That's not good. In the same way that a prophetic culture requires not just prophets to prophesy but for everyone to look for opportunities to prophesy, so we also need to ensure that all Christ-followers are encouraged and equipped to share their faith and be evangelistic. It's noteworthy that Paul tells his apprentice Timothy, who seems to be more gifted in pastoral than evangelistic ministry, that he should nevertheless 'do the work of an evangelist'.[31]

At The Belfrey we're trying to use all the opportunities we can to call people to follow Jesus. So it's rare now for us to gather for public worship and not give this opportunity to people. We find that the more we ask people to start following Jesus, the more positive responses we get! Once they've done this, we encourage them to get baptised, as Jesus commanded in the Great Commission. We don't wait long to do this. If people know they want to follow Jesus for the rest of their life, that is enough. That means we sometimes baptise people on the day they come to faith, or within a week or so. We then get them linked up with others to encourage them and invite them to join a small group to grow as disciples. It's all part of making disciples.

Discipleship

Some churches think that once someone has come to faith there's very little for them to do, apart from come to a church service once a week. That approach is rather like giving birth to a baby and hoping that a once-a-week check-in is all that's needed for it to survive and grow! No, it takes time, love and intentional action to grow and be well-nurtured as a disciple. This is the exciting journey of discipleship.

Discipleship is the daily practice of following Jesus. My basic guide to discipleship, *A–Z of Discipleship* unpacks this in more

detail, explaining that discipleship is following Jesus. It is literally that – going where he goes, saying what he says and doing
what he does. It's not something we just do every now and
then; rather it's a lifestyle that we live all day every day, 24/7.
It's also something that requires practice and discipline.

There are various tools and disciplines that train us well for
a lifetime of discipleship, some of which are unpacked in the
book. These include: generous giving, fasting, regular receiving
of Holy Communion and much more. (If you want to know
more about some of these prayerful disciplines, then try my
A–Z of Prayer.)

In the Great Commission of Matthew 28, Jesus tells his
disciples to go and make more disciples. As such, all discipleship should be missional discipleship.[32] The Antioch church,
as we've been discovering, modelled this so well. But Jesus
didn't just tell his disciples to go and make disciples and baptise. He also told them that they should be 'teaching them to
obey everything I have commanded you' (v. 20) knowing that
his Presence went with them. This teaching ministry – faithfully and effectively communicating the teachings of Jesus in
the power of the Spirit – is crucial to discipleship. This is what
Barnabas and Saul did in Antioch[33] as it became a teaching
centre of renown for the region. Barnabas's pastoral gifts, combined with his and Paul's teaching gifts, helped nurture and
grow the disciples in Antioch.

At The Belfrey we teach regularly and often. At every worship service and in small groups. We encourage people to read
books on discipleship, recognising that disciples who read are
disciples who grow. We use all sorts of means to help nurture
disciples. But the most important thing we do is urge Christ-followers to read or listen to the Bible every day. This is what has

sustained me and grown my faith over the last thirty-plus years and there is no substitute for it, if we want to grow mature disciples in our churches. So, every morning I awaken around 5.15 a.m. and I come downstairs and I set aside the first hour of my day for personal devotions. I read the Bible. I want the first words I take in to be the words of God. I pray and occasionally read a devotional book too. Sometimes I might journal and record what I've been reading and praying, as well as anything significant happening in my own life, or in my family, or in my church family. Before I read the Bible, I ask the Holy Spirit to help me, as the Bible is the Spirit's book and he loves to help us not only understand it but also apply it.

I have used various models of Bible reading over the years. At the moment I read a chapter or two of the Old Testament plus a chapter of the New Testament every day, along with a psalm or proverb. If I do this, I will get through the Bible in about a year and a half. Sometimes, as I read, I will pause to reflect on a passage. I might scribble something down that gets my attention or requires further thought. All this is for my own personal prayers, so I can get to know Christ and his Word better. While occasionally a sermon might emerge from my daily Bible reading, the point of this daily quiet time is not to study for a sermon but to read as an act of devotion. It's how I learn to hear God's voice, understand his ways, discern his will and seek to live each day in his service. I know that daily Bible reading is the main way that I grow as a disciple.

The other way I grow is by spending time with other believers, in worship, prayer, Bible study and fellowship. This is crucial to discipleship, as we're meant to learn and grow together, in community. There's no such thing as a solitary believer, in the Bible. In fact, we need each other much more than most of us realise! We need each other's help, support, challenge, love and prayers – and much more. Following Jesus is the best life, but it's also a tough life, and we have an enemy – the devil – who wants to pick us off. One biblical picture of the devil is that of a lion. We know from wildlife programmes on TV that one of the main ways lions catch their prey is by isolating them from the pack. Once they've managed to do that, they're easy pickings. That's why it's so important that we stay in connection with other believers and find a church and small group in which we can give and receive. It's essential to the nature of discipleship, and it helps us grow.

Leadership

In order to see our region transformed with the good news of Jesus, we need disciples who are not only growing but who can lead. I didn't always think this. I used to think that we just needed people to come to faith and then grow in their love for God and then all would be well. Now I see more clearly than ever that the transformation of people and a region requires investment in leadership development.[34]

Luke, the author of Acts, does not describe in any detail how the church of overflow in Antioch identified, developed and released leaders, although we assume they did, as it's unlikely they would allow people to teach and preach[35] without giving them input and training, and then work with them to grow and improve as leaders. We know they were good at spotting potential because, as we've seen, they sent the young man called John Mark with Barnabas and Saul on their first missionary journey.[36] John Mark was a potential leader who at this stage is described as 'their helper'. Colossians 4:10 informs us that he was the cousin of Barnabas. Despite him leaving them part-way through the journey, with Paul later refusing to take him on the next journey, Paul later commented a number of times on Mark's effectiveness in missionary work,[37] and most importantly Mark went on to write the Gospel of Mark – one of the four accounts of the life of Jesus. That work is one of the most important texts ever penned, influencing not just the church[38] and its future development, but world culture. It came from the pen of John Mark, a man who grew up in Jerusalem[39] and was no doubt impacted by the first church that grew in that city. But let's not forget he was also very much shaped by his missionary experience, having being sent out from Antioch with Barnabas and Saul. That means Mark probably was, at that stage at least, part of the Antioch church. His sending and future writing are further examples of the Antioch church's overflowing influence as they raised up future leaders.

On his second missionary journey from Antioch, Paul saw real potential in a young man called Timothy. He met him and his family at Lystra, noting that the church there 'spoke well of him'.[40] Timothy's family may well have started following Jesus when the church was planted during the first missionary journey.[41] This is the same Timothy who Paul then took with him as the good news of Jesus was brought to Europe, and in whom he invested so much time, care and devotion.[42] It's the same Timothy to whom he wrote two important letters. It's the same Timothy to whom he later entrusted the leadership of the overflowing church in Ephesus.

No one is born a leader. Leaders are made. They're forged on the anvil of experience and shaped by watching, listening,

> No one is born a leader. Leaders are made.

praying, asking questions and practising. Leadership is an art that blossoms as burgeoning leaders are affirmed, encouraged, held to account and given increasing responsibility. Responsibility and leadership go together, so much so that leadership could be simply defined as *responsibility*. If you're not responsible for anyone or anything, then you're not leading.

In his excellent leadership book *Tribes,* Seth Godin asks the question: 'What does a leader look like?' to which he answers:

> I've met leaders all over the world, on several continents, and in every profession. I've met young leaders and old ones, leaders with big tribes and tiny ones.
>
> I can tell you this: leaders have nothing in common.
>
> They don't share gender or income level or geography. There's no gene, no schooling, no parentage, no professions. In other words, leaders aren't born. I'm sure of it.
>
> Actually, they do share one thing in common. Every tribe leader I've ever met shares one thing: the decision to lead.[43]

No one can make you lead. It's ultimately a choice. But behind every Christian leader is a call from God to lead, because God loves to call and raise up leaders. It's one of the main ways he works in the world – through leaders. Because people follow leaders. That's why disciples are especially called to pray for leaders,[44] to support leaders,[45] to respect leaders[46] and honour leaders.[47] And it's why leaders are themselves called to make sure they raise up the right kind of leaders[48] and set them free to lead.[49]

What kind of leaders do we need in the church? Especially in churches of overflow? In this book we've seen that the church of Antioch was particularly strong in the areas of prophecy and teaching, but if we look more closely we actually see the other three leadership roles listed in Ephesians 4:11 also at work. As such after a slow start, the church grew as the *evangelists* got to work (see Chapter 7). Then Barnabas the *pastor* came and encouraged the church (see Chapter 4), adding Saul, a gifted evangelist to help the growth to continue. The increasing numbers of disciples were then well taught – by *teachers* (see Chapter 6) such as Barnabas and Saul, and others too. *Prophets* were also involved; some were itinerant and only stayed a short time, while others remained, so much so that prophecy, with teaching, became marks of this church (see Chapter 5). And then from this church people were sent out for evangelism and church planting. Interestingly, the two main leaders who were sent were Paul and Barnabas. These *apostles* were sent but also returned to update the church (see Chapter 8), establishing Antioch as an apostolic centre – a resourcing church – for the region.

Today, we need to be raising up all of these five kinds of leaders. The fact that Barnabas and Paul fitted into more than one category of leadership is not a problem. It shows us that we don't just have one thing that we're good at! It also shows that over time, and in different contexts, we can adapt and change and find ourselves using gifts and leading in a way that we didn't previously think we were capable of.

As we seek to identify and raise up leaders in today's church, it's good to have the five-fold model of Ephesians 4:11 in mind. It's been mentioned regularly in this book, as I'm convinced it's a great shape for overflow.[50] Of course, it doesn't guarantee success as it's a structure made up of flawed and fallible human beings who make mistakes.[51] But nevertheless, it's a biblical shape that seems to facilitate overflow.

While some would advocate structuring your core leadership around these five ministries, I've considered but not sought to do this at The Belfrey. After all, at Antioch their leadership team wasn't structured that way; Barnabas was content to let it be dominated by prophets and teachers. Rather, as I've sought to raise up leaders and develop teams at The Belfrey, I've tried to have very much in my mind this five-fold shape, to ensure we have a good mix of gifts. It's a useful framework as we pray and work to see new leaders raised up in our day. It's also helpful, of course, to have a diversity of gender, age and race on your team, but not at the expense of these five key roles.

One place at The Belfrey where we constantly need new leaders is in our midweek small groups. We've noticed they often start to grow but then stall at a certain number. Some grow to ten, some to twenty and some even thirty people, but they usually can't then grow any more. There may be practical reasons for this, like not having a home big enough to meet in! That can be solved by multiplying into smaller units. But that won't happen if we don't have people ready to lead these groups. We've also noticed that the bigger the group, the less responsibility and ownership people feel. If, for example, someone has had a tough day at work, they're more likely to skip the group that evening if it's a big group, and they think they might not be missed. So, it's good for groups not to get too big. More positively, there's no better way to grow as a disciple than by leading others. Most people who begin to take leadership responsibility find they take their own discipleship much more seriously. They realise that in order to grow, help and support others, they need to be praying, reading the Bible and modelling well what it means to follow Christ. Therefore, for all these reasons and more, leaders of groups need to keep bringing on new leaders, in preparation for group multiplication.

Raising new leaders is crucial not just when it comes to small groups, but for any new venture in church life. If you want to start a new service, congregation or church plant, you need leaders. Thomas Bandy is right when he says:

> The future of the church in the Twenty First Century will not be determined by planning. It will be determined by leadership development. These leaders may be clergy or laity, and they will probably not care about the designation. They will be risk-takers and adventurers. They will always be wondering what opportunity lies over the next cultural hill. They will be explorers of the unknown. They will be you.[52]

A few years ago, I heard Nicky Gumbel, leader of HTB in London, be asked how many churches his church could plant in one year. He replied that they could plant as many as they had leaders. It seems that Paul took a while to realise this and to create an effective strategy to make it happen. I have been helped by Neil Cole's *Journeys to Significance* in considering this. So, when new churches were planted during Paul's First Missionary Journey it's likely that leaders were not appointed immediately but rather as an afterthought, on the way home on his circular journey, as Paul returned to the churches he'd started.[53] On his Second Missionary Journey, however, Paul took a different approach. He took a larger team, leaving a leader in each new plant to help it get established. So he left

Luke in Philippi,[54] Timothy in Thessalonica[55] and Silas in Berea.[56] But the result was that when he arrived in Corinth, Paul was on his own. So on his Third Missionary Journey, Paul uses a different approach. This time, he goes to Ephesus, which he'd briefly visited during his previous trip and, as he'd done in Corinth, he stays there a long time. He has a team but is seeking this time to raise up leaders from within. He finds them in the harvest fields, as God had previously reassured him by saying, 'I have many people in this city.'[57]

If this developing realisation of how Paul found and developed leaders is correct, then there is something important for us to learn here. Not only is there benefit in investing time, energy, people and prayer in one community to help establish it as a resource church, but most importantly, the leaders for that community and the next are often best found from within. That's why, as we noted in the previous chapter, there's great benefit in churches developing a leadership pipeline to create a regular throughput of leaders. An overflowing and resourcing church is a church developing leadership.

One way we've been doing this at The Belfrey in recent years is through our internship programme. Each year we gather a cohort of young disciples for ten months and invest in them. Not only do they grow in their faith as they are taught and experience many different contexts, but they also grow as leaders as they are increasingly given more responsibility. Some of these interns go on and take on further leadership posts with us or elsewhere. Some go on and are ordained as church leaders. In recent years we've put about a hundred and thirty young people through our internship scheme, and it's proved to be a great leadership pipeline. We are making plans to develop and expand it as we look to raise up more leaders into the future.

Planting

The aim of developing leaders in a resource church is, ultimately, to encourage the planting of more churches. We need to see lots of strong churches overflowing with God's grace and impacting their locality and beyond. This is because the local church is God's main vehicle for changing the world. That's not to say that the Spirit will not use other organisations or people, but in the end the church is, and always has been, God's number one choice to bring his transformative kingdom.

The need for revitalisation and planting, certainly in the UK, is greater than ever. In some ways it feels like we're in a context not dissimilar to the situation in which the church found itself back in the days of Barnabas and Saul when the Antioch church was formed, in the first century. Our post-Christian culture in the West is both secular and yet fascinated by religion, with a multiplicity of gods and world views on offer. There is an enormous and exciting missional need with huge potential for overflowing churches to impact individuals, families, streets and communities. That's why we need to plant churches that plant churches.

We have already considered church planting in Chapter 8 as we looked at the vital role of resource churches. Church plants need to be planned, working closely with denominational leadership and other local church leaders too. They need to start well with a good sending team supporting the planter. They should be covered by much prayer. And their leaders need to be full of faith and backed by their sending church. We see this in Antioch in the way that Barnabas was initially sent and helped by the church in Jerusalem. Today, this support might be financial, at least for a given period of time, and will certainly be relational, with leaders being linked to a supportive network so they don't become isolated and can be mentored and learn from more seasoned leaders. New churches always raise lots of questions for their leaders!

The Diocese of London, which has been leading the way in church planting in the Church of England, has said this about church planting:

> From a certain perspective every Church is the result of a planting programme. At some point in history a conscious effort has been made to establish a congregation, to raise a building, to develop local ministry and mission and to encourage Christian life and discipleship to flourish.[58]

It's easy to forget this. Every church was formed in overflow: in mission, for mission. By strategising, praying and working to see more church planting, churches are returning to their missional roots. I believe God is calling churches across our nation and region to take up this challenge as we advance through these early decades of the twenty-first century.

If we don't revitalise and plant more churches, it's just possible that by the middle of this century there won't be very much of a church left in the UK. However, if we willingly take up this challenge, then I think we'll see the transformation of both localities and regions – including the north of England – that so many of us have been longing and praying for. That's why in the coming years I am prayerfully expecting more and more overflowing churches to emerge. We must not be threatened by them; rather we should encourage and

> I am prayerfully expecting more and more overflowing churches to emerge.

support them, so they can fulfil their biblical mandate and be local churches transforming regions. That way, we will see not just a few churches overflowing with God's grace, but a whole movement of churches across regions, nations and continents. It's what the world needs. That's why the final chapter explores what such a movement might become and urges us to work and pray to see it happen in our day.

Application: Strategising for evangelism, discipleship, leadership and planting

Questions for disciples and church leaders to consider from this chapter:

1. Do you invite friends who are not Christians, to church? Does your church, at services and events, offer an opportunity for people to start following Jesus? If not, why not?

2. What's your plan for ensuring you continue to grow as a disciple? And how are you helping others grow in their discipleship?

3. Who is helping you develop in your gifts and leadership? And who are you raising up as a leader?

4. How can your church more intentionally plant churches that plant churches?

5. Which of these four areas – evangelism, discipleship, leadership and planting, is weakest in your church? And which is your strongest? What are you going to do about this? Pray for the Spirit's help in all this.

Preparing for an Overflow Movement

I was recently sitting in a lecture room with a cohort of church planters. We had been learning about models of church planting and how to plant well and strategically. I was at Asbury Theological Seminary in Kentucky, appreciating the opportunity to study with some fantastic leaders from across the world. Winfield Bevins was now upfront and wanting to give us the big picture – to show how local church planting has always been crucial to the growth and expansion of the worldwide church, so this session was about church planting and missional history to date. Then Winfield said something that got my attention. Having talked about all that was learned by the so-called 'church growth movement' at the end of the last century, he then said that what we need today is not church growth. We don't just need more churches. We don't even need growing churches. What we need is a movement. A movement of God's Spirit. Like those of the past. Like the Methodist movement catalysed by John Wesley. A revival movement that impacts society.

As he spoke my heart leaped. I scribbled down what he was saying and wondered if I might be honoured to be part of something like that in my day. From there we went to join in the weekly service in the chapel, and as I began to sing the Spirit of God came on me, and I began to weep in God's presence. I knew the Spirit was stirring my heart about missional movements. The preacher at the service was a great American Methodist saint, Maxie Dunnam, and his message included references to an awakening presently happening in Cuba, where many are coming to Christ, churches are being started and a move of God's Spirit is taking place.

Again I sensed the Spirit of God speaking to me about a movement which he wants to fan into flame across the nations – and even in my nation and my region. I felt awed and yet a little apprehensive. Convicted and challenged. Encouraged and excited. At the end of the service I asked Maxie to pray for me. In a lovely fatherly way, he took hold of my hands and prayed for me, and for the north of England. He prayed a simple prayer, that in the same way the Lord moved in the past, so he would do it again. I agreed – with a big 'Amen'.

This desire to see a movement of God's Spirit is something I see growing in our day. I see it in the prayers of many. I hear echoes of it in the multiple prophecies being declared of a soon-to-come awakening in the Western world. Yet there have been many declarations of such things over the last century that have not been realised. The church in the UK continues, in general, to decline. But maybe now is the time. Maybe this is the generation. I for one am certainly asking the Lord for such a fresh outpouring of the Holy Spirit in my day. Because we need revival. And I'm convinced, from my prayers and reading of Scripture, that the Lord wants it too. He desires a great awakening of his

Spirit to take place. It happened in days of old, and so there is no reason why it can't happen in the future. If it is to follow the pattern of old, it will come to a large extent through overflowing churches that birth an overflowing church planting movement.

A movement

What is a movement?

There is no agreed definition of a movement, but at its simplest a movement is a group of people with particular aims who want to effect change. In his book, *Marks of a Movement*, Winfield Bevins agrees, simply and succinctly expressing it like this: 'movements are all about change.'[1] There are all kinds of movements, often noted by sociologists, such as social movements, political movements, mass movements and religious movements. What they share in common is a desire for transformation. A group or party or organisation becomes a movement when their aims start to impact beyond themselves and influence culture.[2] That's why overflowing churches are key to helping create a movement of God's Spirit.

Movements have an identity. There's a core cause or particular project behind why they exist. Steve Addison, who's written extensively on Christian movements, considers remaining true to 'Identity' to be crucial to the success of movements.[3] This 'Identity' is at the heart of what they're about. It's about *why* they exist. As a group becomes clear and intentional about pursuing strategy and methods related to their identity, and they begin to grow, so they can increasingly develop momentum and often reach a tipping point when they take off.[4] The church of Antioch, which began as a church of overflow, birthed such a movement of God's Spirit. From Antioch, churches were planted which themselves planted churches, and so a missionary movement began that spread like wildfire across the known world.

Characteristics of church-planting movements

How did this happen? How did this overflowing church of Antioch develop into a movement?

David Garrison, writing in 1999, noted ten characteristics of church-planting movements.[5] These characteristics have since been widely recognised by a variety of missiologists[6] as foundational to such movements, and all feature prominently in the overflowing church of Antioch. If we want to see a fresh movement of God's Spirit, we would be wise to take note of these characteristics and pray for them to be evidenced in our churches today. Each are briefly examined below.

1. Extraordinary prayer

The church in Antioch was a praying church. Church history also shows us that nothing of lasting significance happens without prayer. However, as Garrison explains, 'it is the *vitality* of prayer in the missionary's personal life that leads to its imitation in the life of the new church and its leaders. By revealing from the beginning the source of his power in prayer, the missionary effectively gives away the greatest resource he brings to the assignment. This sharing of the power source is critical to the transfer of vision and momentum from the missionary to the new local Christian leadership.'[7] That's why the prayerful leadership of Barnabas and Saul was so important in Antioch, providing the foundation for the overflowing church-planting movement that later developed. We see this too in other church-planting movements throughout church history – notably in the continuous prayer in the eighteenth and nineteenth centuries of the Moravian church, who sent out church planters across the world. There is much today for us to learn here.

2. Abundant evangelism

The Antioch church, as we know, had good news – indeed *very* good news – to share. They truly believed that the gospel of Jesus was the best news of all time! Those who found faith in Christ at Antioch felt compelled to share this news through word and action and, as a result, others came to faith and through the church-planting movement began by Barnabas and Saul, new churches were started in many cities, towns and villages. John Wesley, the founder of the Methodist movement, had a similar compulsion to share the good news of Jesus which he not only employed as an evangelist but passed on to his Methodist preachers. The result was a huge evangelistic harvest in their day. If we are to see a movement of church planting in our day, we need to be confident in our evangelism and committed to the overflowing and transformative power of the gospel.

3. Intentional church planting

The believers in Antioch spread the good news of Christ not only by evangelising but by starting churches. They did this by particularly targeting larger cities, to establish further resource churches like themselves. That's why churches were directly planted from Antioch in Philippi (to reach Macedonia); in Thessalonica (to impact other parts of Macedonia and Achaia), in Corinth (to influence further into the Achaia area), and in Ephesus (to reach Asia Minor). The disciples at Antioch can take no credit for the church in Rome (which impacted Italy and beyond), except for the influence that Paul later had on Rome through his great epistle and through the time he later spent there. This overflowing influence of the church in Antioch is easily missed, but was crucial for the growth and expansion of the early church. That's why Steve Addison rightly says: 'the church in Antioch was renewed as it looked beyond its own existence for the multiplication of disciples and churches in other key cities. It became a movement, mobilizing people to act without direct supervision, thus heading toward becoming a great-grandparent – trusting God to give generations of descendants.'[8] Wesley used a similar strategy in the eighteenth century, especially at the start of his ministry, by establishing three city bases for his work: in Newcastle, London and Bristol. These became the resource churches from which church planters were sent out to impact their regions. This is why the Church of England – the denomination of which I'm part – is at present intentionally encouraging resource churches to become established and strengthened in key conurbations across the UK.

4. Scriptural authority

The language Luke consistently uses in Acts for the developing church-planting movement, is 'the word spread'.[9] These first Christians genuinely believed that their role was to pass on God's word, found in Scripture. This is what Barnabas and Saul were doing in Antioch. They were faithfully teaching the Bible, as they 'met with the church and taught great numbers of people'.[10] The apostles in Jerusalem had the same priority, so they decided, when challenged over their use of time, that 'we . . . will give our attention to prayer and the ministry of the word'.[11] Today, the Bible must therefore continue to be the foundational tool for church planting. That's why David Garrison says: 'While Church Planting Movements have occurred among peoples without the Bible translated into their own language, the majority had the Bible either orally or in written form in their heart language.'[12] We see this in a huge church-planting movement presently taking place in northern India, through organisations like Jossy Chacko's Empart, where the Bible is taught with simplicity and authority, resulting in thousands of new churches beginning in recent years.[13]

5. Local leadership

As the church in Antioch grew, so local church leadership became the norm there. The reader of Acts 11:19–30 may not see this at first, but as we read on we realise this had to be, otherwise Barnabas and Saul couldn't have gone away for such long periods of time.[14] It may have taken a while for Paul to realise the need to raise up and pass on the leadership, but certainly this is what he did, in time. And it seems that Paul increasingly saw this need to establish local leaders, as he planted churches across the region during his three missionary journeys. Raising leaders was key so that an overflowing movement could be created that grew not by addition, but by multiplication.[15] Three hundred

> Leadership development is the limiting factor in most churches.

and fifty years ago, John Welsey used similar principles in his church-planting movement, and we need to do the same today. It's often noted that leadership development is the limiting factor in most churches and so we need to produce more leaders than we think we need!

6. Lay leadership

Barnabas and Saul were professional ministers who were well-educated. We've seen that Barnabas came from a Levite family[16] and Saul was trained as a Pharisee by Rabbi Gamaliel.[17] But after they were filled with the Spirit and began to evangelise, pastor and plant churches, there is no evidence that they expected the local church leaders to be similarly professionally trained. Leadership was lay. Training was on the job. In fact, church history shows that professionally educated leadership can stifle overflow, causing the movement of the Spirit to slow and come to a grinding halt. As David Garrison says, 'This reliance upon lay leadership ensures the largest possible pool of potential church planters and cell church leaders. Dependence upon seminary-trained – or in nonliterate societies, even educated – pastoral leaders means that the work will always face a leadership deficit.'[18] This is a challenge to those of us today who expect all our leaders to be ordained and professionally educated.

7. Cell or house churches

New churches normally begin organically. It seems that God doesn't wait for a building to be completed before new believers appear. It's normally the other way round! In fact, most new churches start with small groups meeting in homes, and it's only after a while that they gather into larger homes or community buildings and form congregations. While meeting in a designated building has its benefits, giving the church profile in the local community, history shows that it can often slow down the growth. Indeed, one of the reasons why the church in China has exploded over the last fifty years or so has been that it's largely been an underground house church movement. So, when there are too many people to meet in one home, they simply form another church in another home!

We're not sure how the large and growing church gathered in Antioch. When Luke says in Acts 11:26 that 'Barnabas and Saul met with the church and taught great numbers of people', this could have happened in a large public square or outside the city in a field, but it could also have taken place in multiple small group settings, as the two pioneer leaders travelled around, encouraging the believers. Many think it's likely that a mix of the two took place, as had been the case in Jerusalem, where the first believers met both in a large group 'in the temple courts' as well as 'in their homes'.[19]

8. Churches planting churches

If a resource church plants a church, and then the following year the resource church plants another, then we would rightly call that church growth. It is growth by addition. But as we've seen in Chapter 8, it's much more effective to plant churches that plant churches. If resource churches are able to do this, then we begin to see growth by multiplication. This is how movements are formed. This is what happened in Antioch as the overflowing church spilled out into the region and new churches began which also planted new churches. For this kind of multiplication to take place, local believers need to believe that such reproduction is normal and natural – that it can happen! – and that it's God's desire and plan for them. They don't have to wait for external help or particular resources to become available. God will provide all they need. Heidi Baker, leader of Iris Global, teaches this, and to date Iris have planted some 40,000 churches in the African continent over the last twenty-five years, through this overflowing movement of God's Spirit.

9. Rapid reproduction

Church history shows that once a movement begins, the reproduction rate accelerates. The new believers and planters have a sense of urgency about their task of reaching their friends, family and neighbours with the good news, and they want to get on and start new churches. This seems to have been the case in Antioch, as they sent out Barnabas and Saul not just once, but three times! They felt the urge to go. To pioneer. To get on with the task. The result was rapid reproduction. We see this in the church planting pioneered by Pentecostal believers in countries such as Brazil and Argentina in the second half of the twentieth century, where new churches were being formed weekly as pioneer missionaries passionately preached the good news of Jesus and formed churches. We need such passion in the UK church today!

10. Healthy churches

Finally, a movement is normally born from strong, healthy foundations. As the saying goes: healthy things multiply.[20]

Healthy churches normally do the basic things of the faith simply and well. Indeed, they tend to do the kind of things that were practised by the church in Antioch, and that we've seen in this book, namely: evangelism, discipleship, leadership development and church planting. And they often do this in the context of worship, prayer and fasting.

Church history shows that overflowing church-planting movements tend to form simple, healthy churches, unencumbered by bureaucracy or complex structures, which themselves can easily multiply. Such churches are also pragmatic about reproduction, recognising that sometimes churches form but don't grow well. I recall some years ago, when researching the growth of Methodist societies in the eighteenth century, that a significant percentage did not survive after two years. If there weren't signs of life and growth, they were closed and resources invested elsewhere. These pioneers strategically invested long-term only where there were signs of healthy life. That's one reason why the work begun by Wesley wasn't just a ministry, but became a movement. It was a movement of healthy churches.

> Overflowing church-planting movements tend to form simple, healthy churches.

Unique qualities of the Antioch church

So, the Antioch church exemplified all these ten characteristics, providing good foundations for a church-planting movement. As well as these, there were a few other unique factors about the Antioch church that I think were also significant. Indeed, every church community has a few special qualities that are given by the Spirit to help them fulfil God's missional call. So, what were these at Antioch? What were the unique qualities that prepared them so well to be such a key resource church for the region at that time? Three stand out.

1. Multi-ethnic church

The first was that it was a multiethnic church. In fact, it seems to have been the first multiethnic church! In a culturally divided context where most people rarely strayed outside their own racial groups, this modelled something that was attractively countercultural. They demonstrated how the good news of Jesus breaks down social boundaries and is, indeed, a message for all people. This multiethnic nature of the Antioch church was demonstrated and modelled in their leadership team, highlighted in Acts 13:1. There we're told:

> In the church at Antioch there were prophets and teachers: Barnabas, Simeon called Niger, Lucius of Cyrene, Manean (who was brought up with Herod the tetrarch) and Saul.

Simeon was from Niger, in sub-Saharan West Africa, and Lucius was from Cyrene, a city now in Libya. That means they were both Africans. Manean was from somewhere in the Palenstine region, where Herod ruled, and we already know that Barnabas was from Cyprus[21] and Paul from Tarsus.[22] The fact that Luke, the writer of Acts, highlights their ethnicity should not be overlooked. Luke clearly felt it important to record this in the context of describing such a dynamic and overflowing church. In today's increasingly multiethnic context, this is important, as Mark DeYmaz recognises in his helpful book, *Building a Healthy Multi-Ethnic Church*. There he asks: '*So why did the church at Antioch care about the world?* Because the church at Antioch reflected the world!'[23] An ethnically mixed church, both then and today, with leadership that reflects its make-up, is likely to be a healthy church with a strong desire to overflow out beyond its locality.

2. Great leadership

A second unique quality of the Antioch church is that the Spirit brought to them great leaders. We've seen in Part Two that all five leadership roles highlighted by Paul in Ephesians 4:11 functioned well in this church. And these leaders were not just good – they were great! They were bright, gifted and able. Through their individual upbringings and life experiences it looks like they'd been prepared for this season in their life so they could pioneer one of the most exciting churches and church-planting movements in the history of the world! It seems that the Lord knew exactly who was needed to lead this church to fulfil its potential. But they also, as we've seen, trained others, and were keen to see others raised up into leadership.

The core leadership team, as we've noted, was also small. Just five leaders are mentioned in Acts 13:1,2. This means that even though they came from varied backgrounds they were of a size to be able to find consensus and not be held up by the time-consuming decisions that normally go with a larger group.

In today's church, we should similarly expect the Lord to be calling his chosen leaders to the right place, in order to help each church fulfil its divine calling. This should be an encouragement to us, and to church leaders today.

3. Robust discipleship

In Part One we saw that the Antioch church was a church that not only grew in numbers but also in discipleship, particularly through their commitment to worship, prayer and fasting. They invested time listening to the Lord and encouraging each other. They were well-taught by their leaders. And, in particular they generously gave away. They became devoted 'Christians' – people of Christ – and as a result strong disciples were nurtured. These followers of Jesus not only shared the good news with others, but they also modelled it in their lives as they 'remain[ed] true to the Lord', even when there were times of opposition and persecution.[24] This resilience enabled them to stand strong, to stay faithful and to overflow in fruitfulness. While every church wants to grow robust disciples, this was a particularly strong quality of the Antioch church.

So, churches have characteristics. Some of these are unique, and others are shared with other churches that go on to play a part in forming a movement. Garrison's ten qualities of church-planting movements are, I believe, especially helpful for us, as we seek to grow overflowing churches and pray for a fresh overflowing movement of God's Spirit today.

But church history shows us that movements often slow down and fizzle out. Why is this? We will briefly consider this, in the hope that we can be prepared so that future church-planting movements might be sustained and carry on for the long-term.

The rise and fall of movements

Movements rise and fall. Leadership expert and business adviser Jim Collins sees such a rise and fall pattern also in companies. In his book *How the Mighty Fall*, Collins charts five stages in the life of a business or organisation.[25] His five-stage growth and decline process is remarkably similar to the five-stage life-cycle highlighted in movements by Steve Addison. Building on work by sociologists such as Howard Stark and others, Addison summarises the five stages in the life of a movement as:

- Stage 1: BIRTH
- Stage 2: GROWTH
- Stage 3: MATURITY
- Stage 4: DECLINE
- Stage 5: DECAY

This can be diagrammatically represented as shown in figure 1:[26]

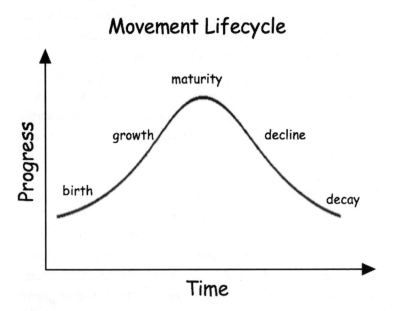

Figure 1

For both Collins and Addison, the most vulnerable time is at the beginning of Stage 3, in the move to maturity. Collins notes that this is when businesses become overconfident and so stray into new markets, failing to do the basic things that previously brought them success. Addison recognises that movements at this stage often become complacent, losing their initial passion, and make poor choices, invariably choosing security over identity, thus sowing the seeds of decline. Both recognise that the key to continued success is a return to essentials. If they don't do this, then to most people the business or movement will look like it's still growing nicely but in reality it's running on momentum – on past rather than present success – and will soon slow and begin to dip into decline.

What does this mean for movements? Does it mean that all movements are destined for decline? Is it inevitable? Collins, writing about companies, answers this very question when he says that his research shows:

that it is possible to build a great institution that sustains exceptional performance for multiple decades . . . In fact, our research shows that if you've been practicing the principles of greatness all the way long, *you should get down on your knees and pray for severe turbulence*, for that's when you can pull even further ahead of those who lack your relentless intensity.[27]

So, the answer is: No – decline is not inevitable. Troubles will come, and when they do, a return to essentials is needed. Both Collins (in business) and Addison (in church-planting movements) agree that the key to sustaining momentum is to stick to basics. To be true to your core identity. To not over-complicate things and to simply and vehemently practice your core principles. You should beware of bureaucracy and the fatigue of institutionalisation and aim to continue to do a few things well.

For as long as the Antioch church did the simple things of the faith – the kind of things highlighted in this book – they grew and had an overflowing impact, and the movement they began prospered. But history unfortunately shows that they floundered. Over time they, and many of the churches they planted, declined and struggled. It is likely that God spoke to them early in this process, calling them back to basics and, particularly, to stay passionate about Jesus. That was the point of most of the New Testament letters – to keep both individual disciples and churches on track and healthy. And in particular the letters from Christ to the seven churches – listed in Revelation chapters 2 and 3[28] – were written to churches planted out of Antioch, through Paul and his companions.[29] However, it is salutary to realise that within a few hundred years there was no church in any of these cities.[30] It is a powerful reminder that there is no place in the church for complacency, and that we always need to be a people of overflow, reaching out in mission, revitalising old churches and planting new ones.

> We always need to be a people of overflow.

New movements

The good news, of course, is that despite the decline of these churches and the movement of which they were a part, God went on to raise up many subsequent church-planting movements, and he's still doing so today. In fact, if we have eyes to see, he is powerfully at work across the world right now. In every continent.

In particular the Lord seems to be attracted to places where he is invited. That's why we need to ask him to come. To come in power and love. To come and bring his kingdom here on earth, as it is in heaven.

I, for one, and the church I lead, want to pray and work with all our passion, to see churches of overflow grow and develop in our region, in expectation that we will see a powerful and healthy church-planting movement again in our day which brings revival to our region.[31] That is our need. That is our hope. That is our desire.

And that is why we will continue to pray, again and again: 'Come, Holy Spirit.'

Application: Preparing for an overflow movement

Questions for disciples and church leaders to consider from this chapter:

1. Which of David Garrison's ten movement characteristics is your church strong in? And in which is it weak?

2. Does your church have any unique qualities that will help you in the mission to which God has called you?

3. Most movements rise and then fall when they become complacent about their identity. What do we learn from this, for ourselves, and our churches?

4. Are you praying for a fresh overflowing movement of God's Spirit in our day? Will you commit yourself to seek God for this? Will you gather with others to pray and work for this? Why not pray: 'Come, Holy Spirit.'

Afterword

One Sunday morning early in 2008, I awoke with a strong sense that I should offer prayer for healing across the day at all the services at St Chad's Church in Woodseats, Sheffield, where I was vicar. I remember getting out my jar of anointing oil, so I could use it to anoint people with oil for healing, as James 5:14,15 encourages leaders to do. As I reached for the jar, I noticed that there was very little oil left. I thought to myself, 'Oh, that will only last for a half a dozen or so people.' But it was all I had, and so I took it to church.

At the first service I prayed for some people, anointing each of them with the oil. I was so focused on the praying that I used the bottle without looking to see how much oil there was, but I think I prayed for about a dozen people at the first service. I then continued praying for people at the next service, using the same jar. After praying for another fifteen or so people, I thought to myself, 'Has the oil run out yet?' So, I looked at the jar for the first time since the start of the day in order to see how much oil was left, and was surprised to see that it was just over half full. I was flabbergasted! I looked again to be sure, and yes, it was at least ten times fuller than it had been at the start of the day.

I stood there wondering if someone, somehow, had taken it and filled it up, but no, I knew that hadn't happened. So, I thanked the Lord for his provision, and used it some more, both at that service and then during the evening service too. I then continued to use that bottle of oil for a whole year, taking it with me when we moved to York, with the oil level always remaining the same. Over the following six months in York I prayed for at least one hundred people – maybe more – using that jar of anointing oil, and the level of oil never once went down. As I prayed and anointed people, many encountered the presence of the Holy Spirit, some receiving healing, others peace and joy and more. I returned from holiday in September 2009 to find that everything in the pockets of my clerical robes had disappeared – including the bottle of oil – never to be seen again. But I will never forget that oil. I recall occasionally getting out a ruler to measure the oil level and every time I did the amount remained exactly the same, at just over half full. It never went down.

I wrote to the Bishop of Sheffield, Jack Nicholls, to tell him the story. He sent me a postcard, replying in his usual succinctly encouraging style, which said: 'Dear Matthew. Thank you for your letter. There's always more oil.'

I smiled when I received the postcard, because what he said is so true! There is always more oil of the Holy Spirit. Despite our imperfections there is always enough. More than enough. Especially when we live and act generously, like our good Father. When we simply follow Jesus, live a life of giving, and encourage our churches to become churches of overflow, there will always be more. More impact. More transformation. More overflow.[1]

> There is always more oil of the Holy Spirit.

Afterword

I pray that this book will encourage and enable many churches in these coming years to become churches of overflow, because it's as we overflow with the Lord's goodness that we'll see new churches planted and, I trust, a fresh movement of God's Spirit in our day.

> It's as we overflow with the Lord's goodness that we'll see new churches planted.

Appendix:
Five-fold Ministry

In this book I have said that the five-fold ministry of apostles, prophets, evangelists, pastors and teachers (of Ephesians 4:11) provides a good shape for ministry in an overflowing church.

In Chapters 4 to 8 I describe each of these five kinds of leaders in more detail. There I take note of their helpful influence on the church in Antioch and how each of these ministries can be of value in the church today – especially in churches of overflow. In summary, apostolic ministry is about establishing, prophetic ministry is about perceiving, evangelistic ministry is about gathering, pastoral ministry is about caring and teaching ministry is about instructing. A missional church needs these roles, and God calls and equips leaders in his church in these areas, in order to equip the wider church for works of service.[1]

In considering each of the five leadership roles, I have noted that there may be some kind of correlation between them and the five love languages, highlighted by Gary Chapman.[2] For example, it would not surprise me for it to be generally true that a teacher, who uses words as a key tool, would receive love through affirming words; that a pastor, who loves people, would enjoy spending time with others; that an evangelist, who is a natural salesman/woman would enjoy receiving gifts; that a prophet, who often senses and feels God's presence, would welcome physical affection, and that an apostle, who likes to get things done, would like practical help. Mapping these five love languages onto the five-fold ministry is not something I have seen done before, and so it would be good if some thorough analysis could be done to see if there is any empirical evidence to validate my hunch that there's a link between the two.

I also note, in Chapters 4 to 8, that the strength of each leadership gift can, if misdirected and misappropriated, become a weakness. I have also noticed that the same is true when it comes to the love-languages. Each has a potential shadow side.[3] For example:

- Apostles are good at pioneering and people-gathering, but their weakness might be enjoying and taking for granted people who serve them. This can lead to an abuse of power and, if taken to an extreme, can result in them becoming a bully.
- Prophets are good at hearing (from God), but their potential weakness is manipulating their prophetic gift for personal gain. I have noted that many prophets, who often physically sense the presence of God, probably enjoy the love language of physical affection. That means they must take particular care not to fall into physical and sexual temptation.
- Evangelists are good at gathering a harvest of souls through their gospel sales pitch. Outside of the church these people would have a tendency to work in marketing, selling things. That's why they value gifts, especially financial gifts. Pushed to an extreme, evangelists can be tempted into financial manipulation. Over the last thirty years we have seen a number

of examples of high-profile evangelists being exposed for financial impropriety. That's why evangelists must take particular care over financial matters.

- When it comes to pastors, they are usually extremely kind and this is often shown in the way they are willing to give much time to people. In response, they love it when others are willing to do the same for them. Their weakness is that their love for people could potentially outweigh their love for God's Word and so they become vulnerable to compromising on biblical truth and, when pushed to an extreme, become open to heresy – that is, doctrine or beliefs that are inconsistent with the Christian doctrine.

- Teachers are good at instructing. As such, they like it when others share affirming words with them, and about them. Their potential weakness is not, like the pastors, compromising truth resulting in potential heresy. Rather it's compromising on love, as they become overly focused on *the task* of teaching at the expense of *the person* being taught. Their teaching can then become legalistic, lacking in grace, which then misses the very heart of the gospel of Jesus Christ.

If I am correct in this, then there are great benefits of each of the five-fold ministries. When we are set free to be the people God has made us to be, then God can use us in wonderful ways. But each leadership gift and role has its weakness too, which

> Each leadership gift and role has its weakness too.

means that wise leaders must seek to be constantly growing and maturing in both their emotional intelligence and self-awareness.

All this can be summarised diagrammatically (Table 1):

Table 1: Leadership roles and their strengths and weaknesses

Leader	Strength	Potential Weakness	Love Language	Weakness When Misused
Apostle	establishing	power	acts of service	bully
Prophet	perceiving	sex	physical affection	manipulator
Evangelist	gathering	money	gifts	exploiter
Pastor	caring	truth	quality time	heretic
Teacher	instructing	love	affirming words	legalist

The weakness of each leadership role should not put us off pursuing our gifts and callings. Rather, it should cause us to stay close to Christ and to stay accountable to others, in the fellowship of the church. Things go wrong when leaders start to become too independent. When they become mavericks. When they think they know better than the church.

This book is essentially about the church. It's about churches of overflow. Church, as I said in the Introduction, is about people. Christ's people. The body of Christ. We are an imperfect people but, in Christ, we are a glorious people who need each other and who, in the power of the Spirit, are commissioned together to bring God's transformative kingdom of heaven here on earth. May we humbly and faithfully fulfil this call in our generation.

> Stay close to Christ and . . . stay accountable.

Further Reading

1 Small Beginnings

On the Early Church, including Acts, Paul and the New Testament Epistles:

Neil Cole, *Journeys to Significance* (San Francisco, CA: Jossey-Bass, 2011).

Michael Green, *Evangelism in the Early Church* (London: Hodder & Stoughton, 1970, 1984).

C. Peter Wagner, *The Acts of the Holy Spirit series*, vol. 1–3 (Ventura, CA: Regal, 1994, 1995).

Tom Wright, *Paul: A Biography* (London: SPCK, 2018).

On St Michael le Belfrey, York:

Matthew Porter, *David Watson: Evangelism, Renewal, Reconciliation* (Cambridge: Grove, 2003).

David Watson, *You Are My God* (London: Hodder & Stoughton, 1983).

On Overflow:

Brian Houston, *There is More* (London: William Collins, 2018).

2 Worship, Prayer and Fasting

On Worship:

James K.A. Smith, *You Are What You Love* (Grand Rapids, MI: Brazos, 2016).

A.W. Tozer, *Whatever Happened to Worship?* (Eastbourne: Kingsway, 1986).

On Prayer:

Mark Batterson, *The Circle Maker* (Grand Rapids, MI: Zondervan, 2011).

Samuel Chadwick, *The Path of Prayer* (London: Hodder & Stoughton, 1931).

Paul Y. Cho, *Prayer: Key to Revival* (Waco, TX: Word, 1984).

Matthew Porter, *A–Z of Prayer* (Milton Keynes: Authentic Media, 2019).

On Fasting:

Mahesh Chavda, *The Hidden Power of Prayer & Fasting* (Shippensburg, PA: Destiny Image, 1998).

Richard Foster, *Celebration of Discipline* (London: Hodder & Stoughton, 1989, 2000).

Matthew Porter, *Spiritual Discipline & Leadership Formation* (Cambridge: Grove, 2005).

Arthur Wallis, *God's Chosen Fast* (Eastbourne: Kingsway, 1968).

3 Giving Away

Heidi Baker, *Learning to Love* (Maidstone: River Publishing, 2012).

Brené Brown, *Daring Greatly* (New York: Penguin, 2012).

Martin Charlesworth & Natalie Williams, *A Church for the Poor* (Colorado Springs, CO: David C Cook, 2017).

Christian Smith & Hilary Davidson, *The Paradox of Generosity* (Oxford: OUP, 2014).

4 Joyful Community – the gift of the pastor

Beni Johnson, *The Happy Intercessor* (Shippensburg, PA, Destiny Image, 2009).

Bill Johnson, *God is Good* (Shippensburg, PA: Destiny Image, 2016).

Eugene Peterson, *The Pastor* (New York: HarperOne, 2011).

Richard Sheridan, *Joy, Inc.* (New York: Portfolio, 2015).

5 Prophetic Culture – the gift of the prophet

On Prophecy:

Alex & Hannah Absalom, *Hearing the Voice of God* (Long Beach, CA: Dandelion Resourcing, 2019).

Shawn Bolz, *Modern Prophets* (Studio City, CA: iCreate Productions, 2018).

Tania Harris, *God Conversations* (Milton Keynes: Authentic Media, 2017).

Bill Johnson, *Releasing the Spirit of Prophecy* (Shippensburg, PA: Destiny Image, 2014).

Kris Vallotton, *School of the Prophets* (Bloomington, MN: Chosen, 2015).

On Culture and Culture Change:

Sam Chand, *Change Your Culture, Change Everything* (Atlanta, GA: Sam Chand, 2017).

Sam Chand, *Cracking Your Church's Culture Code* (San Francisco, CA: Jossey-Bass, 2011).

6 Teaching Centre – the gift of the teacher

Bill Hybels, Stuart Briscoe, Haddon Robinson, *Mastering Contemporary Preaching* (Leicester: IVP, 1989).

Tim Keller, *Preaching* (London: Hodder & Stoughton, 2015).

John Piper, *The Supremacy of God in Preaching* (Leicester: IVP, 1990).

John Stott, *I Believe in Preaching* (London: Hodder & Stoughton, 1990).

7 Evangelistic Confidence – the gift of the evangelist

William Abraham, *The Logic of Evangelism* (Grand Rapids, MI: Eerdmans, 1989).

Robert Coleman, *The Master Plan of Evangelism* (Grand Rapids, MI: Baker, 1963, 1964, 1993, 2006).

J.John, *Calling Out* (Milton Keynes: Word, 2000).

David Watson, *I Believe in Evangelism* (London: Hodder & Stoughton, 1976).

8 Resource Church – the gift of the apostle

Ché Ahn, *Modern-Day Apostles* (Shippensburg, PA: Destiny Image, 2019).

Mike Breen, *The Apostle's Notebook* (Eastbourne: Kingsway, 2002).

Alan Hirsch and Tim Catchim, *The Permanent Revolution* (San Francisco, CA: Jossey-Bass, 2012).

9 Evangelism, Discipleship, Leadership, Planting

On Evangelism: see Further Reading – Chapter 7
On Discipleship:
Robert Coleman, *The Master Plan of Discipleship* (Grand Rapids, MI: Spire, 1987, 1998).

Bobby Harrington and Alex Absalom, *Discipleship That Fits* (Grand Rapids, MI: Zondervan, 2016).

John McGinley, *Mission-Shaped Grace* (East Malling: River Publishing, 2017).

Matthew Porter, *A–Z of Discipleship* (Milton Keynes: Authentic, 2017).

David Watson, *Discipleship* (London: Hodder & Stoughton, 1981).

On Leadership:

Sam Chand, *Leadership Pain* (Nashville, TN: Thomas Nelson, 2015).

Seth Godin, *Tribes* (London: Piatkus, 2008).

Alan Hirsch, *5Q* (Colombia: 100M, 2017).

Bill Hybels, *Courageous Leadership* (Grand Rapids, MI: Zondervan, 2002).

William Porter, ed. *Igniting Leadership* (Ilkeston: Morleys, 2005).

David Pytches, *Leadership for New Life* (London: Hodder & Stoughton, 1998).

Andy Stanley, *Next Generation Leader* (Sisters, OR: Multnomah, 2003).

On Planting:

Winfield Bevins, *Church Planting Revolution,* (Franklin, TN: Seedbed, 2017).

Neil Cole, *Church 3.0* (San Francisco, CA: Jossey-Bass, 2010).

Neil Cole, *Organic Church* (San Francisco, CA: Jossey-Bass, 2005).

Dave Ferguson & Jon Ferguson, *Exponential* (Grand Rapids, MI: Zondervan, 2010).

Craig Ott and Gene Wilson, *Global Church Planting* (Grand Rapids, MI: Baker Academic, 2011).

Ed Stetzer and Warren Bird, *Viral Churches* (San Francisco, CA: Jossey-Bass, 2010).

Tim Thorlby, *Love, Sweat and Tears: Church Planting in East London* (London: Centre for Theology & Community, 2016).

10 Preparing for an Overflow Movement

Steve Addison, *Movements That Change the World* (Smyrna, DE: Missional Press, 2009).

Steve Addison, *The Rise and Fall of Movements* (Atlanta, GA: 100Movements Publishing, 2019).

Winfield Bevins, *Marks of a Movement* (Grand Rapids, MI: Zondervan Reflective, 2019).

Jim Collins, *How the Mighty Fall* (London: Random House, 2009).

Notes

Introduction

1 Habakkuk 3:2.
2 An overflowing church like this is a church fulfilling Jesus' Great Commission which he gave to his disciples, and recorded in Matthew 28:16–20. The Gospels, and the Great Commission in particular, provide the initial Bible foundations for a theology of church planting.
3 As I have researched this, I discover that many others agree, including Mark DeYmaz, who calls it 'the most influential church in the entire New Testament'. Mark DeYmaz, *Building a Healthy Multi-Ethnic Church* (San Francisco, CA: Jossey-Bass, 2007), p. 22.
4 I agree with Ott and Wilson that 'Though the New Testament is not a church planting manual, it does give church planters principles and parameters to guide them in their efforts' and as such there is much to learn today. They helpfully show that some things in the Bible, and especially in Acts, are meant to be *prescriptive*, others *descriptive* and others still carry *representative* value. This third category recognises 'consistent patterns' which are noteworthy. 'By the use of repetition, literary emphasis, and other devices the author makes them stand out as normal (customary, typical)

practices, even if they are not given normative (absolute, author-itative) force.' See Craig Ott and Gene Wilson, *Global Church Planting* (Grand Rapids, MI: Baker Academic, 2011), pp. 39 and 44–6.

[5] Paul first appears in Acts as 'Saul'. The tradition of two names was common at the time. In Acts 13:9 he is travelling with Barnabas on his First Missionary Journey and is described as 'Saul, who was also called Paul'. From then on, Luke (the author of Acts) calls him Paul. For clarity, this book will call him Saul up to that point in time, and Paul afterwards.

[6] Indeed, this book offers something of a biblical basis for church planting, emphasising the importance of resource churches, in-spired by the example of the overflowing church in Antioch. I write not as a theologian or missiologist but as a Bible teacher and church leader. As such the Bible is referenced on multiple occasions in this work (as opposed to rarely in books on church planting that offer a more multidisciplinary approach, such as Stefan Paas's helpful *Church Planting in the Secular West* [Grand Rapids, MI: Eerdmans, 2016]).

Part One: Foundations of Overflow
1 Small Beginnings

[1] The disciples had not yet taken up Jesus' command to 'go and make disciples of all nations' (Matt. 28:19).

[2] 'Tradition speaks of the Antioch church's leadership after the depiction of Acts 13:1. After Peter's ministry, Evodius became the city's first bishop, followed by Ignatius (martyred ca.107 C.E.) . . . Despite several persecutions under Decius (250 C.E.) and Diocletian (303 C.E.), the church experienced enormous growth, and thirty church councils were held at Antioch from the mid-third to the early sixty centuries.' (Craig Keener, *Acts: An Exegetical Commentary*, vol. 2 [Grand Rapids: Baker Academic, 2014], p. 1840).

3   Keener says that 'God's "hand" being with a person can be equivalent to God being "with" him or her in a positive way' (Keener, op. cit., p. 1842).

4   This is what Paul meant when he told his protégé Timothy to 'preach the word and be prepared in season and out of season' (2 Tim. 4:2).

5   A brief summary of the work amongst the Iranians in Stockton can be found in *Evangelism for the Local Church* (Thy Kingdom Come 2018 publication), pp. 20–1. https://www.thykingdomcome.global/sites/default/files/2019-03/JN_11992_TKC_DIY_Evangelism_BookletV25-1.pdf (accessed 27.10.19).

6   'Although Luke had previously recorded Gentile conversions (Acts 8:27–39; 10:1–48), none had occurred on this scale' (Keener, op. cit., p. 1844).

7   To be literally correct, *revival* is not the right term, as it presupposes that there was a work there before which had gone dormant and was now being revived. Clearly this was not the case in Antioch as this was a brand-new work in that city. However, what was happening there for the *first* time had been seen *before* in Jerusalem and would be seen *many* times in the future elsewhere in church history, and is normally termed *revival.* That's why Michael Green says that all outpourings of the Spirit 'derive from this one source' of Pentecost, because 'had the Spirit not been poured out on that first Pentecost, there would have been no later revivals' (Michael Green, *When God Breaks In* [London: Hodder & Stoughton, 2014], p. 31). As such, I am content to use the term *revival* for what later happened in Antioch.

8   See Matthew Porter, *A–Z of Discipleship* (Milton Keynes: Authentic, 2017), pp. 116,157.

9   See, e.g. Mark Stibbe, *Revival* (Crowborough: Monarch, 1998); Brian H. Edwards, *Revival!* (Darlington: Evangelical Press, 1990); Colin Whittaker, *Great Revivals* (Basingstoke: Marshalls, 1984).

10   Source unknown, but widely and commonly attributed to D.L. Moody.

11   Jesus said so, in Mark 1:15 as he called people to 'repent and believe the good news'.

[12] See Romans 12:1,2.

[13] In accordance with Acts 2:47.

[14] Despite all the good things that had been happening in the church in Jerusalem, leadership was needed to help troubleshoot potentially difficult and divisive issues that arose, including the telling of lies (see Acts 5) and how to properly care for the poor (see Acts 6). The Jerusalem church had also sent Peter and John to Samaria (see Acts 8:14) to ensure all was well, as that church began to grow.

[15] See Acts 4:36.

[16] See Acts 4:37.

[17] See Acts 6:1–6.

[18] See Acts 4:36.

[19] See Romans 3:20–24; 2 Corinthians 12:8,9; John 1:14.

[20] This is an example of what Paul later describes to the church in Corinth, when he writes that 'I planted the seed, Apollos watered it, but God has been making it grow' (1 Cor. 3:6).

[21] Downloadable at: http://seniorpastorcentral.com/wp-content/uploads/2016/11/Tim-Keller-Size-Dynamics.pdf (accessed 22.10.19).

[22] See Acts 7:54 – 8:1.

[23] See Acts 9:1–19. Scholars date Saul's conversion between AD33–36.

[24] Tarsus was only 100 miles from Antioch, whereas Jerusalem was about 300, so it also made practical sense to seek out Saul in Tarsus, rather than some other teacher-evangelist in Jerusalem.

[25] See Acts 9.

[26] See Galatians 1:13–24.

[27] Neil Cole thinks this is possibly hinted at in Galatians 1:21 and Acts 15:23,41. See Neil Cole, *Journeys to Significance* (San Francisco, CA: Jossey-Bass, 2011), p. 29.

[28] See Acts 9:27. Cole writes warmly about this episode in *Journeys to Significance*, recognising how much Saul needed a friend at this moment and how Barnabas was used by God to help Saul (see p. 28).

[29] Kris Vallotton, in Bill and Beni Johnson et al, *Spiritual Java* (Shippensburg, PA: Destiny Image, 2012), p. 89.

[30] Words spoken, and recorded by this writer, at *Thy Kingdom Come* 2018 launch event, Bishopthorpe Palace, York, 23 January 2018.

[31] This may well be the same visit Paul describes in Galatians 2:1–10 when he says he went to Jerusalem 'by revelation' (v. 2), presumably referring to the prophetic word from Agabus. This is the view of Tom Wright in *Paul: A Biography* (London: SPCK, 2018), p. 95.

2 Worship, Prayer and Fasting

[1] See Psalm 71:23.

[2] See 1 Corinthians 10:31.

[3] John E. Rotelle, ed., Augustine of Hippo, 'Sermon 34' in *The Works of St Augustine: A Translation for the 21st Century*, Part III – Sermons, vol 11: sermons 20–50 (trans. Edmund Hill; Brooklyn, NY: New City Press, 1990), p. 168.

[4] See 1 Peter 2:5.

[5] Psalm 23:1 (TPT).

[6] See James 4:8.

[7] See Acts 2:46 and 20:20.

[8] Acts 2:42 talks of 'breaking of bread' which most commentators see as an early reference to sharing what became known as the Lord's Supper or Holy Communion or the Eucharist. The Aramaic makes this more explicit which is why The Passion Translation translates this phrase as 'celebrate communion'.

[9] See definition of prayer and a basic introduction to Christian prayer, in Matthew Porter, *A–Z of Prayer* (Milton Keynes: Authentic Media, 2019), p. 1.

[10] Luke 18:1.

[11] Widely attributed to Martin Luther but source unknown.

[12] Church planter and author K.P. Yohannan, who we've had the privilege of hosting at The Belfrey, says 'the devil hates prayer. He hates it more than choir practice, seminars, conferences and Christian concerts. He will do everything in his power to stop

us from engaging in this dangerous activity. In fact, prayer is so destructive to him that he is more than happy to see us choose instead to listen to a sermon, read a Christian book or work for charity' (K.P. Yohannan, *Reflecting His Image* [Carrollton, TX: Gospel for Asia, 2002], p. 98).

[13] Porter, *A–Z of Prayer*.

[14] See my chapter 'F is for Fasting' in *A–Z of Prayer*, op. cit. pp. 43–9.

[15] That's why Jesus, speaking to his disciples in Matthew 6:16 says 'When' you fast rather than 'if' you fast.

[16] See Mark 9:29.

[17] Including Moses, David, Elijah, Ezra, Esther, Darius, Daniel, Jesus and Paul.

[18] Porter, *A–Z of Discipleship*, pp. 25–6.

[19] Others, who for medical reasons are advised not to fast, will omit TV or social media. This is a good thing to do, but is not really biblical fasting, as it doesn't involve the voluntary giving up of food. The giving up of food is key to fasting. When our bodies say 'feed me' we choose, for a limited time, to exercise discipline and say 'no'. Rather than seeking food, we seek God.

[20] Mark Batterson, *The Circle Maker: Student Edition* (Zondervan: Grand Rapids, 2012), p. 152.

[21] Indeed in Richard Foster's seminal book *Celebration of Discipline* (London: Hodder & Stoughton, 1989, 2000), he begins chapter 4 on fasting by saying: 'In my research I could not find a single book published on the subject of Christian fasting from 1861 to 1954, a period of nearly one hundred years' (p. 61).

[22] See Acts 12:25 – 13:3.

[23] Acts 14:23.

3 Giving Away

[1] Wimber taught that 'You only get to keep what you give away.' See John Wimber, *The Way In is the Way On* (Eastbourne: Kingsway, 2007), p. 233.

2   I first became aware of the work of HTB and their desire to plant churches, after reading the book edited by Bob Hopkins, which was a compilation of talks given at the 1991 fourth national day conference on Church Planting in the Church of England, held at their church in Knightsbridge. See George Carey and others, edited by Bob Hopkins with Tim Anderson, *Planting New Churches* (Guildford: Eagle, 1992). That book sparked my interest in church planting, as did Roger Ellis and Roger Mitchell's book published in the same year, *Radical Church Planting* (Cambridge, UK: Crossway Books, 1992), which includes an Appendix written by Sandy Millar, then vicar of HTB, where he says, 'I can only affirm the truth of the New Testament statement that "the more you give, the more you get"! And I'm equally sure that you only get in order that you should give and this process can be continued as long as the Lord allows' (p. 210).

3   See Matthew 6:4.

4   Matthew 6:2 (my emphasis).

5   Brian Houston, *There is More* (London: William Collins, 2018), p. 38.

6   See John 3:16.

7   In fact, this is very much in line with the teaching on generosity found in the wisdom literature in the Bible. See e.g. Proverbs 11:24–31.

8   See 2 Peter 3:8; Ecclesiastes 3:1–8.

9   I was reminded of this recently as I read Erling Kagge's book *Silence*. Kagge is not a follower of Jesus but has learned much through silence. In this lovely and sometimes prophetic book he says: 'We *do* have enough time. Life is long, if we listen to ourselves often enough, and look up' (Erling Kagge, *Silence* [London: Random House, 2017], p. 54).

10   See Genesis 2:2.

11   The sabbath is also a picture of the rest that we find as we put our faith in Jesus Christ. See Hebrew 4:1–4.

12   See, e.g. Alex Soojung-Kim Pang, *Rest* (London: Penguin, 2016), and Cal Newport, *Deep Work* (London: Piatkus, 2016).

13   See, e.g. Exodus 34:21; Deuteronomy 5:12–15; Isaiah 58:13ff; Mark 2:27.

[14] In his chapter on 'Generosity', in *Mission-Shaped Grace*, John McGinley interestingly includes a section on time, reminding us that 'time is precious and people are blessed when we give them time' – see John McGinley, *Mission-Shaped Grace* (East Malling: River Publishing, 2017), p. 121.

[15] R.T. Kendall, *The Presence of God* (Lake Mary, FL: Charisma House, 2011), p. 117.

[16] The clearest example is the story of the widow giving 'all she had to live on', in Luke 21:1–4.

[17] See Matthew 6:33.

[18] See Deuteronomy 12:11.

[19] See 1 Corinthians 16:2; 2 Corinthians 9:7.

[20] See Exodus 35:21; John 6:9.

[21] See Luke 5:6,7.

[22] See, e.g. Psalm 146:5–9.

[23] See, e.g. Deuteronomy 15:7,8; Proverbs 22:22,23; Jeremiah 22:3; Micah 6:8; James 2:15,16.

[24] See www.tearfund.org (accessed 22.10.19).

[25] See Matthew 6:10.

[26] See Acts 11:30.

[27] See Luke 12:32.

[28] See 1 Corinthians 4:2.

[29] See, e.g. Psalm 139:7ff; 1 Corinthians 6:19; Colossians 1:27–29.

[30] See Genesis 1:28.

[31] See Titus 1:6–8.

[32] See Acts 2:44,45; Luke 14:28.

[33] See 1 Peter 4:10.

[34] See Proverbs 3:9; Luke 16:11.

[35] See Genesis 1:1 and 1:2.

[36] See, e.g. Psalm 144:12ff.

[37] See John 3:16.

[38] See Joel 2:28,29; John 3:34.

[39] See e.g. Proverbs 3:10.

[40] See Acts 13:1.

Part Two: Leadership for Overflow
4 Joyful Community: The gift of the pastor

[1] Hebrews 1:9.
[2] Nehemiah 8:10.
[3] Richard Sheridan, *Joy, Inc.* (New York: Portfolio, 2015), p. 9.
[4] In John 16:19–24 Jesus speaks three times of joy. The first (in v. 20 – 'your grief will be turned to joy') describes the sadness the disciples were to experience at his death, compared with the joy they'd know at his resurrection. The second (v. 22 – 'no one will take away your joy') is a reminder that true joy is an undiminishing gift from Jesus that's not dependent on circumstances. The third (v. 24 – 'Ask and you will receive, and your joy will be complete') shows that while Jesus' joy can't decrease (see v. 22), it can increase! That happens, for example, as a result of answered prayer, testimony and thanksgiving.
[5] See 1 Peter 1:8,9.
[6] R.A. Torrey, *Why God Used D.L. Moody* (Chicago, IL: The Bible Institute Colportage Ass'n / Fleming H. Revell Company, 1923), pp. 51–9.
[7] Bill Johnson with Jennifer A. Miskov, *Defining Moments* (New Kensington, PA: Whitaker House, 2016), p. 51.
[8] Sam Chand, *Cracking Your Church's Culture Code* (San Francisco, CA: Jossey-Bass, 2011), p. 46.
[9] Acts 11:23.
[10] Porter, *A–Z of Discipleship*, p. 29.
[11] This point is well-made and demonstrated by Peter Scazzero in chapter 1 of his *The Emotionally Healthy Church* (Grand Rapids, MI: Zondervan, 2003, 2010). The chapter is entitled: 'As Go the Leaders, So Goes the Church'.
[12] John 3:3.
[13] Ephesians 1:18.
[14] Heidi Baker, *Birthing the Miraculous* (Lake Mary, FL: Charisma House, 2014), p. 117.
[15] John 5:19.

16 Romans 8:37.

17 Rick Warren, *The Purpose Driven Life* (Grand Rapids, MI: Zondervan, 2002), p. 177.

18 See Mark 10:18; Matthew 7:11.

19 See e.g. Psalm 119:68; 1 Chronicles 16:34; Nahum 1:7.

20 See Romans 8:9.

21 See Ephesians 5:18.

22 See Luke 11:13.

23 Bill Johnson, *When Heaven Invades Earth* (Shippensburg, PA: Destiny Image, 2003), p. 75.

24 For example, in chapter 13.

25 Heidi Baker, *Compelled by Love* (Lake Mary, FL: Charisma House, 2008), p. 35.

26 2 Corinthians 6:2.

27 Johnson, *When Heaven Invades Earth*, p. 53.

28 In Acts 11:23.

29 See Acts 14:27.

30 Acts 15:3.

31 Acts 15:4.

32 See Acts 15:12.

33 E.g. in Hebrews 11.

34 2 Timothy 1:7.

35 1 John 4:18.

36 Whereas Paul was adamant that the priority of the gospel was paramount, and that Mark's past record meant he should be left behind.

37 Eugene Peterson describes himself as a 'pastor' and helpfully says this: 'As pastor my work [is] to pray and teach and preach these Holy Scriptures into the lives of mothers and fathers raising their children, farmers in the wheat fields, teachers in the classrooms, engineers building bridges, sergeants and colonels keeping watch over our national security and not a few arthritic octogenarians in nursing homes' (Eugene Peterson, *Christ Plays in Ten Thousand Places* [London: Hodder & Stoughton, 2005], p. 63).

38 See Alan Hirsch, *5Q* (Colombia: 100M, 2017), p. 111.

[39] Letters to Malcolm Chiefly on Prayer by CS Lewis © copyright CS Lewis Pte Ltd 1963, 1964.

[40] Matthew 6:10.

[41] Romans 14:17.

[42] Beni Johnson, *The Happy Intercessor* (Shippensburg, PA: Destiny Image, 2009), p. 179.

5 Prophetic Culture: The gift of the prophet

[1] See 1 Corinthians 14, especially v. 5.

[2] Like the prophetic message brought by Haggai, recorded in Haggai 1:13, where God said 'I am with you'. Although general in nature, that was just the word they really needed to hear at that time!

[3] Acts 2:37.

[4] Isaiah 48:5.

[5] Chand, *Cracking Your Church's Culture Code*, p. 103.

[6] See Acts 15:32–33.

[7] Kris Vallotton, *The School of the Prophets* (Bloomington, MN: Chosen, 2015), pp. 142–43.

[8] 1 Corinthians 14:1.

[9] 1 Corinthians 14:3.

[10] See Matthew 7:7–12.

[11] Numbers 12:6.

[12] David Watson, *I Believe in the Church* (London: Hodder & Stoughton, 1978), p. 258.

[13] John 10:27 (NRSV).

[14] See e.g. John 1:1.

[15] Psalm 119:105; 2 Timothy 3:16.

[16] Proverbs 25:2.

[17] Bill Johnson, *Dreaming with God* (Shippensburg, PA: Destiny Image, 2006), p. 60.

[18] See 1 Samuel 3.

[19] See Genesis 41:32.

[20] In Genesis 37.

[21] In Genesis 41.

[22] Alex and Hannah Absalom agree. In their excellent book, *Hearing the Voice of God*, they see these three aspects of prophecy to be crucial, including key chapters on each. See Alex & Hannah Absalom, *Hearing the Voice of God* (Long Beach, CA: Dandelion Resourcing, 2019).

[23] In 1 Timothy 1:18 Paul urges Timothy to do this, saying 'that by recalling [prophecies] you may fight the battle well'.

[24] Isaiah 45:21.

[25] Hirsch, *5Q*, p. 106.

[26] 1 Thessalonians 5:19–22.

[27] In 1 Corinthians 14:1.

[28] Gary Chapman in his popular books about love languages says that in essence people experience love in one of five ways: through words of affirmation; acts of service; receiving gifts; quality time and physical touch. See e.g. *The Five Languages of Love* (Chicago, IL: Moody Press, 1995, 2015). In the Appendix to this book I make a tentative suggestion that there may be a link between the five-fold ministry and Chapman's five love languages.

[29] Ephesians 2:20.

[30] Which is why all five are mentioned together by Paul in Ephesians 4:11,12: 'Christ himself gave the apostles, the prophets, the evangelists, the pastors and teachers, to equip his people for works of service.'

6 Teaching Centre: The gift of the teacher

[1] As defined in my *A–Z of Discipleship*, op. cit.

[2] See e.g. John 4:31.

[3] http://www.belfrey.org/talks.html (accessed 22.10.19).

[4] https://matthewporter.blog (accessed 22.10.19).

[5] https://churchleaders.blog (accessed 20.10.19).

[6] See, for example, Andrew Wilson's helpful blog at: http://thinktheology.co.uk/blog/article/whats_the_difference_between_preaching_and_teaching (accessed 20.10.19).

7 See 2 Timothy 4:2.

8 See Ezra 7:10.

9 See Proverbs 4:20,21.

10 I now keep this electronically, on Evernote. See evernote.com (accessed 20.10.19).

11 See Colossians 3:16, which suggests a number of creative ways that God's Word can be communicated.

12 See Proverbs 17:22.

13 See Proverbs 12:18.

14 See Luke 11:34 which, amongst other things, is about seeing and visualising well.

15 See Acts 17:22, which shows Paul's good understanding of his audience.

16 See James 1:22.

17 See Mark 1:15.

18 Hirsch, *5Q*, p. 112.

19 See e.g. Romans 9:30.

20 Ephesians 4:15.

7 Evangelistic Confidence: The gift of the evangelist

1 An 'evangelist' is someone especially gifted in evangelism – that is, telling people the good news of Jesus.

2 Romans 1:16.

3 John 14:6.

4 Hirsch, *5Q*, p. 106.

5 This is what Peter says disciples need to be prepared for. See 1 Peter 3:15.

6 John 4:39.

7 Luke 2:38.

8 Luke 24:10.

9 Like the apostles in Acts 5, who on their release from incarceration and having been told not to speak in the name of Jesus, 'never

stopped teaching and proclaiming the good news that Jesus is the Messiah' (Acts 5:42)!

[10] Hirsch, *5Q*, p. 108.

[11] Acts 1:8 says: 'you will receive power when the Holy Spirit comes upon you; and you will be my witnesses in Jerusalem, in all Judea and Samaria, and to the ends of the earth.'

8 Resource Church: The gift of the apostle

[1] Matthew Porter, *The Missiological Influence of David Watson on Evangelicalism in the Church of England* (MA Dissertation, University of Sheffield, 2000). This was written up in a more popular form in Matthew Porter, *David Watson: Evangelism, Renewal, Reconciliation* (Cambridge: Grove, 2003).

[2] Since David Watson came to York in 1964 and grew the work at St Cuthbert's and then planted into St Michael le Belfrey in 1973, the church has done many things that have helped resource others, from developing leaders, training others, producing resources, encouraging people to serve on strategic groups and committees, to sending people. However, this was not particularly planned or part of an intentional strategy. Developing and realising more of a focused resource church vision and strategy is now both our desire and our plan. It's what we pray and work for. This is all for the sake of overflow. In 2012, when few people were using the phrase 'resource church', I blogged about it in a post called 'Becoming a Resource Church' – see https://matthewporter.blog/2012/06/20/becoming-a-resource-church/ (accessed 28.8.19).

[3] I would argue that generosity is essential to discipleship. After all, Jesus taught generous giving in his basic discipleship teaching in the Sermon on the Mount – see Matthew 6:2. John McGinley agrees, including it as the first key 'missional practice' in his book *Mission-Shaped Grace* (East Malling: River Publishing, 2017), p. 115ff. When a body of believers learns to be generous together,

and this is modelled and taught by its leaders, then there is no stopping the overflowing impact of that community.

[4] Luke 11:1.

[5] See Ric Thorpe, 'City-Centre Resource Churches: A Guide', online article dated June 2015: http://www.churchgrowthrd.org.uk/UserFiles/File/Resourcing_Mission_Bulletin/June_2015/02._City_Centre_Resource_Churches.pdf (accessed 5.2.19).

[6] According to Peter Brierley of Brierley Consulting, a 'larger church' in the UK is a church of 350+ people. See: https://static1.squarespace.com/static/54228e0ce4b059910e19e44e/t/5853fbba37c581f51a120efe/1481898946199/FUTURE_FIRST_Issue+44+MAY+2016.pdf (accessed 5.2.19).

[7] In the Church of England with its parish system, planting can only be done into another parish through establishing a new church and is usually done by way of a 'Bishop's Mission Order' (BMO). Revitalisation, which is planting into an existing church, does not require a BMO, but does need careful coordination and strategising with the bishop to ensure the appointment of the new leader and process is done properly and appropriately.

[8] As has been seen in many examples in the Diocese of London and now in various cities and towns across the UK.

[9] According to the writer to the Hebrews 3:1, Christ is 'our apostle' – the one who was sent-out for us. All apostolic leadership is a response to Jesus and a continuation of the ministry he began before he ascended to heaven.

[10] Alan Hirsch and Tim Catchim, *The Permanent Revolution* (San Francisco, CA: Jossey-Bass, 2012), p. 98.

[11] E.g. Paul, Peter, James and John.

[12] After noting the importance of the original twelve apostles and writers of the New Testament, Steve Addison recognises that there was: 'Another wider group, also known as apostles, [who] shared this call to go into all the world and make disciples. They were pioneer church planters, but they did not share the Twelve's status as authoritative witnesses to the resurrected Lord.' (See Steve

Addison, *The Rise and Fall of Movements* [Atlanta, GA: 100Movements Publishing, 2019], p. 52).

[13] Ott and Wilson, *Global Church Planting*, p. 89.

[14] See Romans 16:7.

[15] See 1 Thessalonians 1:1; 2:6.

[16] See Philippians 2:25. Note that many English translations describe '*apostolos*' here as 'messenger'.

[17] See Romans 16:7. Interestingly, most scholars think Junia was a woman.

[18] Hirsch, *The Permanent Revolution*, p. 99.

[19] See Acts 13:5.

[20] Acts 13:13.

[21] See Mark 6:7; Luke 10:1.

[22] And, indeed, recorded three times: directly by Luke in Acts 9:1–19; and twice more as he records Paul's own recollections of the incident, in 22:1–21 and 26:12–23.

[23] I think Luke similarly describes the call of Peter (in Luke 5:1–11) as a model *discipleship* calling, with key discipleship themes standing out such as: obedience; teamwork; wonder; mission and commitment. Steve Addison agrees that Peter is presented as 'the first' disciple and apostle; see Steve Addison, *Pioneering Movements* (Downers Grove, IL: IVP, 2015), where Chapter 3 is entitled 'Peter, First Among the Apostles'. See: https://matthewporter.blog/2016/02/27/5-marks-of-discipleship/ (accessed 28.9.19).

[24] Paul (as he was later known) sometimes introduced himself as both 'servant of Christ' and 'apostle' – see e.g. Romans 1:1.

[25] See 2 Timothy 3:12.

[26] See John 10:10.

[27] See 1 Peter 1:6,7.

[28] Acts 9:16.

[29] See 2 Timothy 3:11.

[30] Ché Ahn, *Modern-Day Apostles* (Shippensburg, PA: Destiny Image, 2019), p. 48.

[31] See Hirsch, *The Permanent Revolution*, pp. 102–4.

[32] Acts 13:49.

[33] E.g. through the work of Empart, led by Jossy Chacko. See Jossy Chacko, *Madness* (Croydon: Empart, 2016). See also impart.org.uk (accessed 22.10.19).

[34] E.g. through the work of Iris Ministries, led by Heidi and Rolland Baker. See Rolland & Heidi Baker, *Always Enough* (Grand Rapids, MI: Chosen, 2002, 2003). See also irisglobal.org (accessed 22.10.19).

[35] Heidi Baker, *Learning to Love* (Maidstone: River Publishing, 2012), p. 87.

[36] For more on this, see Chapter 10 on the lifecycle of movements.

[37] Interestingly, one of the final chapters in Winfield Bevins' book, *Marks of a Movement* is entitled: 'Movements Can be Messy'. Winfield Bevins, *Marks of a Movement* (Grand Rapids, MI: Zondervan Reflective, 2019), Chapter 8.

[38] Acts 15:39.

[39] One good outcome of this, which is often overlooked, is that two teams were sent out. God was able to turn this disagreement for some good, with a lesson about the value of multiple teams perhaps learned by Paul, as later this seems to have become part of his approach to reaching the regions surrounding Corinth and Ephesus.

[40] See e.g. 2 Timothy 4:11.

[41] This date and suggestion comes from Tom Wright in *Paul: A Biography*, p. 144.

[42] Galatians 2:13.

[43] Hirsch, *5Q*, p. 102.

Part Three: Strategies for Overflow
9 Evangelism, Discipleship, Leadership, Planting

[1] See Acts 2:41.

[2] See Acts 4:4.

[3] See Acts 6:7.

4 See Acts 5:16; 9:26–31.

5 See Acts 8:1.

6 See e.g. Acts 11:1–18.

7 See Acts 16:6–10.

8 See Philippians 4:14–19.

9 Paul writes about this in 1 Thessalonians 1:6–8.

10 See 2 Corinthians 8:1–5.

11 See 2 Thessalonians 1:3,4.

12 See Acts 18:1ff; 1 Corinthians 3:6.

13 See Acts 18:11,18. Indeed Paul uses the word 'overflow' as he encourages this church to continue to 'sow generously', writing: 'The service that you perform is not only supplying the needs of the Lord's people but is also overflowing in many expressions of thanks to God' (2 Cor. 9:12).

14 See 1 Corinthians 3:6.

15 See 1 Corinthians 16:1–3; 2 Corinthians 8 – 9.

16 This could be suggested from Acts 18:19.

17 See Acts 18:18 and 18:24ff.

18 See Acts 19:1–10.

19 1 and 2 Timothy are written to encourage Timothy in his leadership of this important church. See comment on this endnote 15 of Chapter 10.

20 See Colossians 1:7.

21 See Colossians 4:11–13.

22 See Romans 16:1–16.

23 See 2 Timothy 4:6–8.

24 See Romans 16:3,7.

25 See Romans 12:9 – 13:10, and also 15:23–33.

26 See Romans 15, especially vv. 14–22.

27 Neil Cole, *Church 3.0* (San Francisco, CA: Jossey-Bass, 2010), pp. 108–10.

28 Matthew 28:19.

29 There have been many definitions of evangelism offered over the years. One that I find helpful is this one, often used by David Watson at The Belfrey: 'Evangelism is the presentation of the claims of Christ in the power of the Spirit to a world in need by a church in

love' (Evangelism Group of 1978 'Anglican International Conference on Spiritual Renewal'. See *A New Canterbury Tale: The Reports of the Anglican International Conference on Spiritual Renewal Held at Canterbury, July 1978* [Nottingham: Grove, 1978]).

30 A number of surveys in recent years show that people in the UK would, for example, come to church, if invited. See e.g. http://news.bbc.co.uk/1/shared/bsp/hi/pdfs/03_04_07_tearfund-church.pdf (accessed 28.8.19).

31 2 Timothy 4:5.

32 That's why John McGinley's book on discipleship is called *Mission-Shaped Grace.* See John McGinley, op. cit.

33 In Acts 11:26; 13:1; 15:35 and probably in 14:28.

34 In their excellent book, *Viral Churches*, Stetzer and Bird cite Bob Logan, who said to them 'that leadership development is the limiting factor in most churches'. See Ed Stetzer and Warren Bird, *Viral Churches* (San Francisco, CA: Jossey-Bass, 2010), p. 86.

35 As they did in Acts 15:35.

36 See Acts 13:1–5.

37 See Colossians 4:10; Philemon 24; 2 Timothy 4:11.

38 And probably being a source for at least two of the other four Gospel writers.

39 His mother's home is mentioned in Acts 12:12. It was the house where the Jerusalem church prayed after Peter was arrested.

40 Acts 16:2.

41 See Acts 14:8–20.

42 See e.g. 2 Timothy 3:10ff.

43 Seth Godin, *Tribes* (London: Piatkus, 2008), p. 123.

44 See 1 Timothy 2:2.

45 See 1 Timothy 5:17.

46 See 1 Thessalonians 5:12,13.

47 See Hebrews 13:17; 1 Peter 2:17.

48 See 1 Timothy 3:1–10.

49 See Acts 14:23.

50 Alan Hirsch in his excellent book *5Q* goes further, essentially saying, I think, that it's the *best* structure for overflow.

[51] In this book I have suggested that *apostles* should take care not to abuse power (see Chapter 8), that *prophets* might have a particular weakness regarding sexual immorality (see Chapter 5) and that *evangelists* should be aware of a desire for material gain (see Chapter 7). These three 'sins' of money, sex and power are often recognised as the classic three temptations for leaders. See Richard Foster, *Money, Sex & Power* (London: Hodder & Stoughton, 1985).

With regard to the other two types of leaders mentioned in Ephesians 4:11, namely *pastors* and *teachers*, theological pragmatism is a potential weak spot of *pastors* (see Chapter 4) who might find themselves so concerned to show love that they compromise on the truth of Scripture, especially with regard to ethics and morality. As for *teachers*, they should especially take care not to fall into legalism (as noted in Chapter 6). I am grateful to my friend and former colleague, Greg Downes, for some fascinating conversations around these matters in recent years. For a summary of this thinking, see the Appendix at the end of this book.

[52] In a lecture given by Thomas Bandy and cited by Revd Dr Pablo A. Giménez. For more on Bandy, see his *Spirited Leadership* (St Louis, MO: Chalice Press, 2007).

See https://www.slideshare.net/drpablojimenez/moving-off-the-map-congregation-mission-assessment-cma (accessed 11.9.19).

[53] See Acts 14:21–25.

[54] The text reverts from 'we' to 'they' when Paul leaves Philippi (see Acts 16:40), indicating that Luke stayed there. Toward the end of the third journey, when Paul passes through Philippi on his way to Jerusalem, the story becomes 'we' again (see Acts 21:5,6) and remains so until the end of Acts.

[55] See Acts 17:10.

[56] See Acts 17:14.

[57] Acts 18:10.

[58] https://www.london.anglican.org/kb/church-planting/ (accessed 12.1.18).

10 Preparing for an Overflow Movement

[1] Bevins, *Marks of a Movement*, p. 27.

[2] Dave and Jon Ferguson agree, but challenge the notion that movements – especially missional church movements – need to be large. They start small. With one person. See Dave Ferguson & Jon Ferguson, *Exponential* (Grand Rapids, MI: Zondervan, 2010).

[3] Steve Addison, *The Rise and Fall of Movements* (Atlanta, GA: 100Movements Publishing, 2019), p. 30.

[4] Malcolm Gladwell has popularised this notion of 'tipping points' in his bestselling book *The Tipping Point* (New York: Little, Brown, 2000).

[5] Paper produced by David Garrison, 'Church Planting Movements' (Midlothian, VA: WIGTake Resources 1999), pp. 33–6.

[6] Including Neil Cole, in *Church 3.0*, pp. 70–1; Winfield Bevins, in Church Planting lectures given at Asbury Theological Seminary in July 2019; Bryan Collier, author of *The Go-To Church* (Nashville, TN: Abingdon Press, 2013).

[7] Garrison, 'Church Planting Movements', p. 33.

[8] Addison, *The Rise and Fall of Movements*, pp. 105–6.

[9] See e.g. Acts 6:7; 13:49; 19:20.

[10] Acts 11:26.

[11] Acts 6:4.

[12] Garrison, 'Church Planting Movements', p. 34.

[13] See Jossy Chacko, *Madness*.

[14] As they did in Acts 11:30 and 13:3ff.

[15] In his fascinating book *Journeys to Significance*, Neil Cole writes extensively about this adaptation and change in strategy by Paul, as seen in Acts and his letters, as he increasingly aims to raise up local leaders. See Cole, *Journeys to Significance*, especially pp. 74–8 and 108–9. Interestingly, Cole does not address why, then, Paul puts Timothy, a man from Lystra (Acts 16:1) in charge of the church in Ephesus. Perhaps one reason might be that Paul wanted leaders who he knew and really trusted to be leading the resource

churches. As we've seen, these churches were particularly strategic, providing a base for regional planting, and that there were times, like when Barnabas was sent to Antioch, when the best leader was from outside. If this is correct, then it shows that a flexible approach is nevertheless important, and the need to be guided by the Holy Spirit in choosing leaders (see Acts 14:23) is paramount.

16 See Acts 4:36.

17 See Acts 22:3.

18 Garrison, 'Church Planting Movements', p. 35.

19 See Acts 2:46.

20 Source unknown.

21 See Acts 4:36.

22 See Acts 9:11.

23 Mark DeYmaz, *Building a Healthy Multi-Ethnic Church*, p. 23.

24 See Acts 11:23. Paul certainly experienced persecution at Antioch, and so it's likely that this was also the experience of others in the church too – see 2 Timothy 3:10,11.

25 See Jim Collins, *How the Mighty Fall* (London: Random House, 2009). His five stages are: Stage 1: Hubris Born of Success; Stage 2: Undisciplined Pursuit of More; Stage 3: Denial of Risk & Peril; Stage 4: Grasping for Salvation; Stage 5: Capitulation to Irrelevance & Death.

26 Diagram used by permission, see Steve Addison, *The Rise and Fall of Movements*, p. 28.

27 Collins, *How the Mighty Fall*, p. 119.

28 For more on these chapters in Revelation, see the excellent commentary in the Tyndale New Testament Commentary (TNTC) series by Ian Paul, *Revelation* (London: IVP, 2018).

29 Depending how you read Acts 18:9, the church in Ephesus was begun either directly or indirectly by Paul. Certainly Paul felt he was the spiritual father or grandfather of Ephesus, and as such we can say that the church was planted from Antioch. The other Revelation churches are not named in Acts as being directly planted by Paul or his companions, and so probably were begun from Ephesus, as that church shared the good news across their region

and started churches (see Acts 19:10). If this is correct then all the seven churches of Revelation were either children or grandchildren of the overflowing church of Antioch.

[30] All the letters to the seven churches in Revelation include areas of weakness that needed addressing, otherwise their lampstand, symbolising the presence of Christ, would be removed (see e.g. Rev. 2:5). It seems that some did address these issues, at least for a time, with Neil Cole noting that the church in Ephesus was revived after the Revelation letter and was later led by Bishop Onesimus – the runaway slave who became a living example of the grace of God in action. See Cole, *Journeys to Significance*, pp. 130–31.

[31] Stuart Murray, writing as a British Baptist, ended his 2008 book on church planting by saying something similar when he wrote: 'church planting is crucial for the health and future of the church and our participation in God's mission. It is too important to be left to enthusiasts. Directly or indirectly, strategically or locally, full-time or part-time, in planting teams or in support roles, hundreds of thousands of us could become involved. And that might just galvanize a movement after all.' See Stuart Murray, *Planting Churches* (Milton Keynes: Paternoster, 2008), p. 222.

Afterword

[1] Overflow is a significant theme in the Bible. Here are some further scriptures all about overflow (that haven't already appeared in this book) which show overflow to be God's desire for disciples, the church and for humanity. He truly is a God of overflow!

Overflow in unlikely places (e.g. in the desert)

Psalm 65:11,12

'You crown the year with your bounty, and your carts overflow with abundance.

The grasslands of the wilderness overflow; the hills were clothed with gladness.'

Overflow of praise and worship

Psalm 119:171

'May my lips overflow with praise, for you teach me your decrees.'

Overflow of provision

Joel 2:24

'The threshing floors will be filled with grain; the vats will overflow with new wine and oil.'

Overflow of prosperity

Zechariah 1:17

'This is what the LORD Almighty says:

"My towns will again overflow with prosperity and the LORD will again comfort Zion and choose Jerusalem."'

Overflow of hope

Romans 15:13

'May the God of hope fill you with all joy and peace as you trust in him, that you may overflow with hope by the power of the Holy Spirit.'

Overflow of love

1 Thessalonians 3:12

'May the Lord make your love increase and overflow for each other and for everyone else, just as ours does for you.'

Appendix: Five-fold Ministry

[1] Ephesians 4:11–16.

[2] See endnote 28 to chapter 5 and endnote 51 to chapter 9.

[3] Neil Cole is one of the few authors who note this. In his excellent book *Primal Fire*, each of his chapters on the five gifts of Ephesians 4:11 include a section on the shadow cast by each leader. See Neil Cole, *Primal Fire: Reigniting the Church with the Five Gifts of Jesus* (Bonita Springs, FL: Tyndale Momentum, in association with Mark Sweeney & Associates, 2014).

Index

Index

A–Z of Prayer

Building strong foundations for daily conversations with God

Matthew Porter

A–Z of Prayer is an accessible introduction that gives practical guidance on how to develop a meaningful prayer life. It presents twenty-six aspects of prayer to help you grow in your relationship with God, explore new devotional styles and deepen your daily conversations with God.

Each topic has a few pages of introduction and insight, an action section for reflection and application and a prayer to help put the action point into practice. There are also references to allow further study.

978-1-78893-062-8

A-Z of Discipleship

*Building strong foundations for
a life of following Jesus*

Matthew Porter

A–Z of Discipleship is an accessible introduction to the
understanding and practice of the Christian faith. It presents
twenty-six aspects of discipleship to help you grow in your
relationship with God, connect with church and live as a
follower of Christ in contemporary culture.

Each topic has a few pages of introduction and insight, an
action section for reflection and application and a prayer
to help put the action point into practice. There are also
references to allow further study.

978-1-78078-456-4

Our Precious Lives

Why telling and hearing stories can save the church

Steve Morris

In a world of increasing social fragmentation and loneliness, *Our Precious Lives* demonstrates how listening to others can be transformational in creating a sense of belonging. Inspiring stories are grounded by practical ideas to put storytelling at the heart of the church, and questions in each chapter encourage us all to glimpse more of God, revel in our uniqueness and realize that we all have something valuable to offer as his followers.

Underpinned by practical pastoral experience, this is a book full of quirky and unexpected life stories that open us up afresh to the beauty of life and our God.

978-1-78893-079-6

Mission in Marginal Places

The Stories

Paul Cloke & Mike Pears (Eds)

The Mission in Marginal Places book series aims to provoke new understandings about how to respond to a very basic question: how might Christians respond to the Spirit's invitation to participate in God's love for the world, and especially in places of suffering and healing, of reconciliation and justice?

The third book, *The Stories*, is an exploration of the processes and practices of 'storying' mission; of listening to others and then telling appropriate stories about interconnected lives.

978-1-78078-185-3

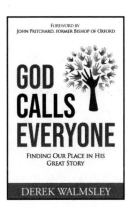

God Calls Everyone

*Finding our place in
his great story*

Derek Walmsley

An accessible and helpful guide for anyone who is trying to
discern what their vocation might be, from those who are
seriously thinking about becoming a vicar or minister to anyone
thinking about what they can contribute to the work of the
Kingdom in a non-ordained capacity.

The uniqueness of this book is that it centres around an overview
of the whole Bible story. The reader is then invited to take part
in God's story, and what he is doing, rather than asking what
they can do for God. Questions at the end of each chapter allow
the reader to reflect, think through the characteristics/attributes
needed for serving God, and ultimately help them to discover
their part in God's story. An accessible book for everyone, written
in a quirky and engaging way, this is a joyous celebration of God
calling us all to be part of his story.

978-1-78893-108-3

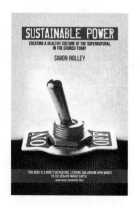

Sustainable Power

Creating a healthy culture of the supernatural in the church today

Simon Holley

The fascinating story of one church community's journey into faith, and a template for the miraculous and living in the reality of the kingdom of God. Simon Holley is the pastor of the King's Arms, a church in Bedford. As he and others in the church learn to hear God and trust that he will keep his promises, they find themselves in exciting encounters with his power both inside the church and while going about their day-to-day lives.

From nearly twenty years of reaching out for more of God's blessings while keeping his feet firmly on the ground, Simon shares simply and honestly what he and his church have learned.

978-1-86024-884-9

WILLIAM PORTER
Foreword by Malcolm Duncan

The Forerunner Cry

*Preparing our lives for Jesus'
return*

William Porter

Talking about the end times can often seem confusing with many differing interpretations held by Christians. But one thing is absolutely clear – Jesus is coming back as a conquering king. So how would we live our lives if we really believed that Jesus was coming soon?

The Forerunner Cry combines a balanced and insightful look at end-times events with a practical guide on how the certainty of Jesus' return should impact the way Christians live now.

978-1-78893-033-8

Finding Our Voice

*Unsung lives from the Bible
resonating with stories from today*

Jeannie Kendall

The Bible is full of stories of people facing issues that are still surprisingly relevant today. Within its pages, people have wrestled with problems such as living with depression, losing a child, overcoming shame, and searching for meaning. Yet these are not always the stories of the well-known heroes of faith, but those of people whose names are not even recorded.

Jeannie Kendall brings these unnamed people to vibrant life. Their experiences are then mirrored by a relevant testimony from someone dealing with a similar situation today.

Finding Our Voice masterfully connects the past with the present day, encouraging us to identify with the characters' stories, and giving us hope that, whatever the circumstances, we are all 'known to God'.

978-1-78893-037-6

Authentic

We trust you enjoyed reading this book from Authentic. If you want to be informed of any new titles from this author and other releases you can sign up to the Authentic newsletter by scanning below:

Online:
authenticmedia.co.uk

Follow us: